MACKIE'S

BOLTON DIRECTORY,

WITH

ALMANACK,

For 1849

9780907511175,
ISBN

BOLTON :

PRINTED BY R. M. HOLDEN, STATIONER, &c.,

13, MEALHOUSE-LANE.

1848.

LIST OF ADVERTISEMENTS.

CONTENTS OF DIRECTORY.

⁎ Those names printed in *Italics* are the first of every letter.
MIS-PRINT.. Page 42, for " Hall," read "HILL," Boiler Maker.

To the Subscribers of the Bolton Directory.

GENTLEMEN,—Now that my work is completed, I return you my most sincere thanks for the ready, cordial, and extensive assistance you have given me.

The knowledge that so many had, on faith, subscribed for copies of my proposed Directory, emboldened me to make it, even more than originally designed, a book of local and general information.

The best guarantee that I can give of its accuracy, is a statement of the fact, that I have spent nearly three months in collection of the materials; and that every line has been inspected by myself and other parties likely to discover errors.

The very small price at which it is published would not make it remunerative, were it not for the hopes I cherish, that a Directory, so cheap and so comprehensive in its particulars, will not be objected to as an *annual* favorite, more easily produced by the same party in the second year than in the first.

I am, Gentlemen,

Your obliged Servant,

A. MACKIE.

Bolton, 29th Decr. 1848.

The "BOLTON ADVERTISER"

WOLSTENHOLME'S SHEFFIELD HOUSE, No. 20, OXFORD-STREET, BOLTON,

IS THE PLACE FOR

GOOD, SUBSTANTIAL, AND CHEAP ARTICLES.

S. WOLSTENHOLME, returns his hearty thanks for past favours, and desires to make known that he has on hand the following Goods.—Penknives, Pocketknives, Razors, and Scissors.

In the **HOUSE-KEEPING DEPARTMENT:**—Fenders, Fire Irons, Tea and Coffee Pots, Tea and Table Spoons; New Knives to match Old Forks; Ivory, Black-tip, Bone, Buckhorn, or any other kind of Handle may be had by sending one for pattern.

S. W, has an ESTABLISHMENT in SHEFFIELD; and all orders intrusted to him will have prompt attention paid to Quality and Price. Parties purchasing Sets of Ivory, or other handled Table Cutlery, may have their Names or Club Stamped upon them

In the **WORKING-TOOL DEPARTMENT** S. W., solicits the following Tradesmen to inspect his Stock :—

Joiners,	Sawyers,	Chair Makers,	Brush Makers,
Carpenters,	Cabinet Makers,	Shoe Makers,	Coopers, and any wanting
Millwrights,	Pattern Makers,	Cloggers,	Cheap and Good Tools.
Wheelwrights,	Coach Makers,	Glaziers,	
		Carders,	
		Curriers,	
		Butchers,	
		Basket Makers,	

Cart Springs, Patent Cart Arms, and Cast Steel, in great variety, always on hand.

☞ *Remember !—The SHEFFIELD HOUSE, Oxford-st., Bolton.*

RICHARD CARLING,
BRUSH MANUFACTURER,
Behind No 11, Cheapside, Bolton,

Brushes Wholesale and Retail. Brushes made of the best materials, for Bleachers, Printers, Mills, &c, at moderate prices.
A GOOD STOCK ALWAYS ON HAND.

MACKIE'S
BOLTON ALMANAC,
AND
GENERAL AND LOCAL INFORMANT,
For 1849;
BEING THE FIRST AFTER LEAP YEAR, AND THE TWELFTH OF THE REIGN OF HER PRESENT MAJESTY.

CONTENTS:

*** Advertisement Index, and List of Carriers, see cover.

BOLTON:

R. M. HOLDEN, Printer, "Bolton Advertiser Office," 13, Mealhouse-lane.

Eclipses During 1849.

1. An annular Eclipse of the SUN, February 22nd; invisible at Greenwich.
2. A partial Eclipse of the MOON, March 8th; visible at Greenwich. Commences 11h. 25m,; middle, 12h. 25m, on the morning of the 9th; ends 2h. 25m, (mean time at Greenwich.
3. A total Eclipse of the SUN, August 18th; invisible in Europe; visible in Africa, Australia, and the Indian Ocean.
4. A partial Eclipse of the MOON, September 2nd; invisible at Greenwich, because ending before the rising of that planet.

Law Terms.—1849.

Hilary Term begins January 11th—ends January 31st.
Easter Term begins April 16th—ends May 8th.
Trinity Term begins May 22nd—ends June 12th.
Michaelmas Term begins Novr. 2nd—ends Novr. 26th.

Common Notes for 1849.

Golden Number 7	Solar Cycle 10	Roman Indiction 7
Epact 6	Dominical Letter .. G	Julian Period.. 6562

CORRESPONDANCE OF THE YEAR 1849 WITH ANCIENT ERAS.

Roman Year .. .. 2602 Julian Period 6562
From the First Olimpiad .. .. ..2625 Death of Alexander, (3d month of).. 2172
From the era of Nebonasser .. ..2597 Dioderian or Martyrs, (24th Cohiac).. 1565
From the era of Abraham (4th mon. of) 3864 Year of the World (Jewish account)
Year of the World (Alexandrian acct.) 7340 | 25 Thebet 5609

The Year 5610 of the Jewish era commences on September 17th, 1849.
Ramadan (month of abstinence observed by the Turks) commences July 22, 1849.
The Year 1266 of the Mahomedan era commences November 17th, 1849.

Banks.

BANK OF BOLTON, Deansgate.—London Agents, Barclay, Bevan, and Co.

The Bank of Bolton grant Letters of Credit on the following places:—

London,	Cheadle,	Oldham,	Wigan,
Liverpool,	Glossop,	Preston,	Stafford,
Manchester,	Hanley,	Rochdale,	Lancaster,
Ashton-under-Line,	Hyde,	Stockport,	Kirkby Lonsdale,
Bury,	Leek,	Staleybridge,	Ulverstone,
Blackburn,	Market Drayton,	Warrington,	Macclesfield.
Burslem,	Nantwich,		

Also, Drafts on London without charge of stamp.

JOHN DARBYSHIRE, Manager; Residence, Lightbounds, Halliwell.
ADAM FERGUSON, Accountant; Residence, Blackburn road, L. Bolton.

HARDCASTLE, CROSS, & Co., Deansgate.—London Agents, Jones, Lloyd, & Co. Letters of Credit granted on the following places: London, Liverpool, Manchester, Blackburn, and Wigan.

SAVING'S BANK, Market-st.—JOHN MAWDSLEY, Esq., Manager.
Open on Saturdays only, from Half-past Two till Four; and from Six to Eight.

LANCASHIRE COUNTY & BOROUGH MEMBERS.

N. Lancashire—John Wilson Patten, James Heywood.
S. Lancashire—William Brown, Alexander Henry.
Ashton—C. Hindley.
Blackburn—J. Pilkington, J. Thornley.
Bolton—John Bowring, LL. D., Stephen Blair.
Bury—Richard Walker.
Clitheroe—M. Wilson.
Lancaster—T. Greene, R. B. Armstrong.
Liverpool—Sir Thomas Birch, E. Cardwell.
Manchester—Hon. T. M. Gibson, John Bright.
Oldham—W. J. Fox, J. Duncuft.
Preston—Sir G. Strickland, C. P. Greenfell.
Rochdale—W. S. Crawford.
Salford—J. Brotherton.
Warrington—Gilbert Greenall.
Wigan—Col. Lindsay, R. A. Thicknesse.

January.—31 *days*.

First quarter, 2nd, 7h, 38m. morning
Full .. ..8th, 10 50 aftern.
Last quarter,16th, 6 54 morning
New .. ..24th, 10 3 morning
First quarter, 31st, 4 42 afternoon

1	1	M	Circumcision
2	2	Tu	Gen. Wolfe born, 1727
3	3	W	Day 7h, 52m. long
4	4	Th	Twilight ends 6, 2
5	5	F	Sun rises 8, 8.—sets 4, 5
6	6	S	*Epiphany.*—Twelfth Day
7	7	—	*1st. Sunday after Epiphany*
8	8	M	Galileo died, 1642
9	9	Tu	Sun sets 4, 9
10	10	W	Archbp. Laud bhd. 1645
11	11	Th	Hilary Term begins
12	12	F	Day breaks 6, 1
13	13	S	Camb. Lent Term begins
14	14	—	*2nd Sunday after Epiphany*
15	15	M	Oxford Lent Term begins
16	16	Tu	Spenser, the poet, d. 1599
17	17	W	Twilight ends 6, 13
18	18	Th	Houses of York and Lan-
19	19	F	[caster united, 1486
20	20	S	Amer. Ind. acknlgd. 1783
21	21	—	*3rd Sunday after Epiphany*
22	22	M	Lord Bacon born, 1561
23	23	Tu	William Pitt died, 1806
24	24	W	Frederic the Gt. b. 1712
25	25	Th	Conversion of St. Paul
26	26	F	Sun ris. 7, 50—sets 4, 39
27	27	S	Mozart born 1756
28	28	—	*4th Snnday after Epiphany*
29	29	M	George III. died, 1820
30	30	Tu	K. Charles I. behd. 1649
31	31	W	Hilary Term ends

THE following statement shows the distribution of the soil of Great Britain in statute acres :—

	Total	England	Wales	Scotland	British Islands
Arable and Gardens.	13,746,950	10,252,800	890,570	2,493,950	109,630
Meadows, Pastures, and Marshes.	20,650,740	15,379,200	2,226,430	2,771,650	274,060
Waste Land capable of Improvement.	10,500,000	3,454,000	530,000	5,950,000	166,000
Incapable of Improvement.	13,454,799	3,256,400	1,105,000	8,523,930	569,469
Total in Statute acres.	57,952,489	32,342,400	4,752,000	19,738,930	1,119,159

Is it right that the people should be without work while there are upwards of ten millions of acres of waste land capable of improvement, yet allowed to lie barren?

MONTHLY NOTICES.—JAN. 6, Half-yearly dividends on some of the species of Stock become due. 8th.—Fire Insurance due at Christmas must be paid on or before this day or the Policy becomes void.

THE QUESTION.—A very pious Presbyterian used always to say, when he met the General Assembly of his church, " Now brethren, how near can we come to doing what is right, and keep together !" A poor editor may as well say, every day when he sits down to his task, " Now, my dear skin and bones, how much truth can we say and live."—*Chronotype.*

The *Bolton Advertiser* is Published on the 1st of every month.

February.—28 days.

Full .. ..7th, 11h, 15m. morning
Last quarter, 15th, 4 2 —
New .. ..23rd, 1 29 —

32	1	Th	Corn Laws expire [day
33	2	F	Purification. Candlemas-
34	3	S	Wilkes expld. H. of Com.
35	4	—	*Septuagesima Sunday* [1769
36	5	M	Sun ris. 7, 21.—sets 4, 50
37	6	Tu	Dr. Priestley died 1804
38	7	W	Day increased 1h. 40m.
39	8	Th	Mary Queen of Scots bhd.
40	9	F	Day breaks 5h. 30m [1587
41	10	S	Queen Victoria mar. 1840
42	11	—	*Sexagesima Sunday*
43	12	M	Lady Jane Grey bhd. 1555
44	13	Tu	Cellini the sculptor d.1570
45	14	W	Captain Cook killed 1779
46	15	Th	Jervis's Victory 1797
47	16	F	Melancthon born 1497
48	17	S	Sun rises 7, 1.—sets 5, 9.
49	18	—	*Quinquagesima Sunday*
50	19	M	Galileo born 1564.
51	20	Tu	*Shrove Tuesday.*
52	21	W	*Ash Wednesday*
53	22	Th	Eclipse of the sun, invisible
54	23	F	Sir. J. Reynolds d. 1792
55	24	S	Revolution in Paris 1848
56	25	—	*1st Sunday in Lent.*
57	26	M	Bonaparte es. f. Elba. 1815
58	27	Tu	Day increased 2h, 40m.
59	28	W	Sun ris 6, 46.—sets 5h, 38

Miscellaneous.

War has destroyed more kingdoms than it has saved, and will always produce far greater evil than it will prevent.—*Sharon Turner.*

Hints to Speakers.—A rasp is an excellent instrument, but not to shave with.

Nothing conduces more to health than abstinence and plain food.

The excesses of youth are drafts upon old age, payable thirty years after date, with interest.

Some people substitute physic for exercise, do you ?

So long as alcohol retains its place among sick patients, so long there will be drunkards.—*Dr. Massey.*

Drunkards are like grasshoppers; whilst they sing over their cups in summer, they starve in winter; and, for a little vain merriment, shall find sorrowful reckoning in the end.—*Burton.*

Life discloses many painful pictures, but none more distressing than a scene of domestic love blighted by intemperance.—*Thomas Beggs.*

With regard to food, clothing, habitations, workshops, and a thousand other minor points, our population are only just beginning to be awake.—*Thos. Beggs.*

Swords and guns are formidable weapons, but even the consequence of these are less to be dreaded than the generally unrestrained viciousness of the human heart.—*J. Livesey.*

In Venice there is a Coffee-house which is said not to have been closed day or night for one hundred and fifty years.

"Wisdom garnishes riches, and shelters poverty."—*Socrates.*

MONTHLY NOTICES. A yearly tenant must take care that he gives notice to quit his premises half a year before the time of the expiration of the current year of his tenancy. If, by agreement, a quarter's notice is to be sufficient, the notice must expire with the tenancy, if that is yearly.

POISONS. When you have reason to suppose that you have swallowed a poisonous substance, and proper medical assistance is not at hand, take an emetic. This may be done almost instantaneously by swallowing a cupful of warm water mixed with a teaspoonful of mustard. If you have not any dry mustard in the house, you are almost sure to have a mustard pot, and a quantity out of that put into the water will soon empty the stomach. As mustard may thus prove of so much use, it should never be wanting in any house; but even should there be no mustard at hand, warm water by itself forms a tolerably efficacious emetic.

March.—31 days.

Changes.
First quarter, 2nd, 0h, 3m, morning
Full .. .. 9th, 1 2   „
Last quarter.. 17th, 0 38   „
New .. ..24th, 2 5 afternoon
First quarter, 31st, 6 58 morning

60	1	Th	St. David's Day
61	2	F	Wesley died 1791
62	3	S	Waller born 1605
63	4	—	*2nd Sunday in Lent*
64	5	M	Corregio died 1534
65	6	Tu	Michael Angelo born 1474
66	7	W	Day increased 3h, 24m.
67	8	Th	Visible Eclip. of the Moon
68	9	F	Peace between Gt. Britain
69	10	S	[and Lahore 1846
70	11	—	*3rd Sunday in Lent*
71	12	M	Chelsea Hos. founded 1682
72	13	Tu	Day breaks 4h, 20m,
73	14	W	Admiral Byng shot 1757
74	15	Th	Julius Cæsar stbd. B.C. 44
75	16	F	Day 11h. 48m, long
76	17	S	St. Patrick's day
77	18	—	*4th Sunday in Lent*
78	19	M	Le Brun born 1739
79	20	Tu	Sir Isaac Newton d. 1727
80	21	W	Archbp. Cranmer bt. 1556
81	22	Th	Battle of Alexandria 1801
82	23	F	Kotzebue as. by Sand 1819
83	24	S	Queen Elizabeth d. 1603
84	25	—	Lady Day. *5th Sun. in Lent*
85	26	M	Sun ris. 5, 47.—sets 6, 20
86	27	Tu	Peace of Amiens 1802
87	28	W	Raffaelle born 1483; died
88	29	Th	Swedenborg d. 1772 [1520
89	30	F	Cambridge Term ends
90	31	S	Oxford Term ends

"The servant of the Lord must not strive."

William Hutton, of Birmingham, says, in one of his works: "The reader will be surprised when I tell him, that during my stay in Scarbro', I never tasted porter, ale, tea, coffee, wine, or any kind of liquors, and yet, at four score, I can with ease walk thirty miles a-day."

Strange inconsistency, when man makes his works of more importance than himself.—*T. Beggs.*

"The true Shekinah is 'man.'"—*Saying of St. Chrysostom.*

Man's life never was a sport to him, but a stern reality; altogether a serious matter to be alive.—*Thomas Carlyle.*

The use of tobacco is a criminal indulgence, unbecoming the professors of the wisdom of God.—*Dr. J. Hamilton.*

It can never be lawful for a righteous man to go to war whose warfare is righteousness itself.—*Lactantius.*

Passive courage is the resolution of a philosopher; active, the ferocity of a savage.—*Soame Jenyns.*

For 300 years christian and soldier were incompatable. What has united them? certainly not a clearer understanding of the gospel.

A Turkish porter will, on an average, carry ten hundred weight: all the Turkish porters are water drinkers.

"In the bottle, discontent seeks for comfort; cowardice, for courage; and bashfulness for confidence."—*Dr. Johnstone.*

The best security, and cheapest defence of nations, is a moral population.

The Appetites are syrens which sing only to deceive, and charm only to destroy: he who listens to them is certain of being shipwrecked in the end.—*Dr. Dwight.*

MONTHLY NOTICES.—*March 1st.* Auditors and Assessors of Boroughs to be elected. 25th. Overseers to be appointed this day, or within fourteen days after. The accounts of those whose year has expired must be verified by them on oath before a magistrate within fourteen days, and be delivered to their successors. 28th. Elections of Guardians under the Poor Law Act, of which day the Board of Guardians are to give thirteen whole days notice in some newspaper generally circulated in the Union.

DEATH is not that terrible thing which we suppose it to be. It is a spectre which frights us at a distance, but which disappears when we come to approach it more closely.—*Goldsmith.*

The *Bolton Advertiser* is Published on the 1st of every month.

April.—30 days.

MOON'S CHANGES.

Full .. .. 7th, 3h, 49m, afternoon
Last quarter 15th, 7   7   ,,
New .. ..22nd, 11   54   ,,
First quarter, 29th, 2   17   .,,

91	1	—	*Palm Sunday*
92	2	M	Bat. of Copenhagen 1801
93	3	Tu	Bishop Heber died 1806
94	4	W	Oliver Goldsmith d.1774
95	5	Th	Maunday Thursday [Day
96	6	F	*Good Friday.* Old Lady
97	7	S	Sun ris. 5,23—sets 6,40
98	8	—	*Easter Sunday*
99	9	M	Lord Bacon died, 1626
100	10	Tu	Grotius born, 1583
101	11	W	Canning born, 1770
102	12	Th	Day 13h, 35m long
103	13	F	Vaccination intro. 1796
104	14	S	Otway the poet d. 1685
105	15	—	1*st Sunday after Easter*
106	16	M	Buffon died, 1788
107	17	Tu	Franklin died, 1790
108	18	W	Ox. & Cam. Eas.T. begins
109	19	Th	American War com. 1775
110	20	F	Span. Fleet des. by Blake
111	21	S	Day increased 6,25[1657
112	22	—	*2nd Sunday after Easter*
113	23	M	Shakspear b. 1564d.1616
114	24	Tu	Sun ris. 4, 49—sets 7,12
115	25	W	Princess Alice born 1843
116	26	Th	David Hume born, 1717
117	27	F	Gibbon born, 1737
118	28	S	Chaucer died, 1434
119	29	—	*3rd Sunday after Easter*
120	30	M	First stone Lon. Uni. laid [1827.

Wine and strong drink have drown'd more than the sea; and the teeth of intemperance have slain more than the sword.

Malt liquor occasions obstructions, inflamations of the lungs, which are brought on by the indigestible nature of strong ale.—*Dr. Buchan.*

Happy is he who considers water his best drink.—*Dr. Paris.*

A drunken man will fight with a turnip.—*Russian Proverb.*

Example, like the sun, makes no noise; yet moves, and every where leaves the affect of his beams.—*Dr. Styles.*

As water is in chief the universal drink of the world, so it is the best and most salubrious.—*Sir John Floyer.*

To set the mind above the appetite, is the end of abstinence, is the ground-work of virtue.—*Dr. Johnstone.*

The most just war is odious and detestable.—*St. Augustin.*

What sculpture is to a block of marble, education is to the mind.

Take care not to go to the brink of vice, lest you fall down the precipice.

The greatest of all faults is, to believe that we have none.

The spirit of war endangers the freedom and liberties of any nation.

While we are warriors, with all our pretensions to civilization, we are savages.—*Dr. Knox.*

Of all absurdities, that of going to war for the sake of getting trade, is the most absurd.—*Dean Tucker.*

The laws of God are superseded by war; theft is no longer stealing, nor killing, murder.

Temperance Societies have encouraged a revision in men's habits.—*Thomas Beggs.*

At a recent meeting in Cork, Father Matthew declared, "that no single individual teetotaler had fallen a victim, either to famine or pestilence:" a text that requires no sermon.

MONTHLY NOTICES.—*April 5th,* Returns for making assessment of taxes are delivered soon after this.   Persons making the returns rate themselves for the persons and articles liable to taxes kept and used by them between the 5th April, 1848, and this day.   Dividends on certain species of Stock also become due.   8th.   Fire Insurance due 25th March must be paid on or before this day.

I have lived to know that the great secret of human happiness is this— never suffer your energies to stagnate.   The old adage of ' too many irons in the fire,' conveys an abominable falsehood; you cannot have too many— poker, tongs, and all, keep them all going.—*Dr. Adam Clarke.*

𝕸ay.—31 *days.*

MOON'S CHANGES.

Full .. .. 7th, 7h, 6m, morning
Last quarter, 15th, 10 30 „
New .. ..22nd, 7 36 „
First quarter, 28th, 11 23 afternoon

121	1	Tu	Union Eng.with Sct.1607
122	2	W	Sun ris. 4, 35—sets 7,22
123	3	Th	Clocks introduced, 1368
124	4	F	Dr.Isaac Barrow d. 1677
125	5	S	Bonaparte died, 1821
126	6	—	*4th Sunday after Easter*
127	7	M	Socrates died B. C. 399
128	8	Tu	Easter Term ends
129	9	W	Corp. and Test Acts repd
130	10	Th	Battle of Lodi,1796[1828
131	11	F	Earl of Chatham d. 1778
132	12	S	Earl Strafford bhd. 1641
133	13	—	*Rogation Sunday*
134	14	M	Vaccin. fst.app.by Jenner
135	15	Tu	Length of day 15,32[1796
136	16	W	Amer. dec. war ags. Mex.
137	17	Th	Ascension day [1846
138	18	F	Bonaparte dec. Emp.1804
139	19	S	Anne Boleyn behd. 1536
140	20	—	*Sun. after Ascension Day*
141	21	M	Sun rises 4,5—sets 7,50
142	22	Tu	Trinity Term begins
143	23	W	Battle of Ramilies, 1706
144	24	Th	Queen Victoria b. 1819
145	25	F	Paley died, 1845
146	26	S	Oxford Easter Term ends
147	27	—	*Whit Sunday.* Cam.Term
148	28	M	[divides at midnight
149	29	Tu	Rest.of King Charles II.
150	30	W	Ox. Trin. T. begins[1660
151	31	Th	Rubens died, 1640

THE FIELD OF WATERLOO.—The field of Waterloo is now rich in waving corn, ripening for the sickle of the husbandman. What a scene it must have been when death was the reaper, and gathered his thousands of sheaves to the garner of the grave! And what a scene will it be again, when the trump of the archangel shall awake the sleepers that repose beneath its clods, and the mighty armies that day annihilated, shall start up to life upon the plain on which they fell! I never heard a sermon so impressive as the silence that reigned around me on the field of Waterloo. I could not but connect a contemplation of their everlasting destinies with a remembrance of the thousands of dead upon whose dust I trod. The Eternity that seemed to open there upon my view, peopled with the spirits of the slain, was an awful scene. The bitterness of dying on the field of battle the widows' cries, the orphans' tears—the agonies of surviving friendship—were all forgotten. I only saw the immortal soul hurried unprepared, and perhaps blaspheming, into the presence of its God! I shuddered at the contemplation, and felt how deadly a scourge, how bitter a curse is War! Amid the repose which mankind once more enjoy, let it be the care of England to cultivate the arts of peace. Let her pour the balm of the Gospel into the wounds of bleeding nations. Let her plant the Tree of Life in every soil, that suffering kingdoms may repose beneath its shade, and feel the virtue of its healing leaves, till all the kindreds of the human family shall be bound together in one common bond of amity and love, and the warrior shall be a character unknown but in the page of history.—*Dr. Raffles.*

SELF-MADE MEN.—Columbus was a weaver. Franklin was a journeyman printer. Sixtus V. was employed in herding swine. Ferguson and Burns were ploughmen. Æsop was a slave. Homer was a beggar. Defoe was an hosier's apprentice. Hogarth, an engraver on pewter pots. Ben Jonson was a bricklayer. Porson was the son of a parish clerk. Akenside was the son of a butcher—so was Wolsey. Cervantes was a common soldier Halley was the son of a soapboiler. Arkwright was a barber. Blackstone and Southey were the sons of linen-drapers. Crabbe, a fisherman's son. Keats, the son of a livery stable-keeper. Buchanan was a farmer. Canova, the son of a mason. Captain Cook began is career as a cabin-boy. Haydn was the soon of a poor wheelwright. Hogg was a shepherd. The list might be extended. Genius, talent, skill, and greatness of character, are confined to no rank. The world's most eminent men have generally issued from the cottage.

The *Bolton Advertiser* is Published on the 1st. of every month.

June.—30 days.

152	1	F	Poussin born 1594
153	2	S	Riots in London 1780
154	3	—	*Trinity Sunday*
155	4	M	Sun ris. 3, 50.—sets 8, 9
156	5	Tu	No real night this month
157	6	W	Ariosto died 1553
158	7	Th	Corpus Christi [1824
159	8	F	New London bridge com.
160	9	S	Reform Bill passed 1832
161	10	—	*1st Sunday after Trinity*
162	11	M	Length of day 16h. 30m.
163	12	Tu	Trinity Term ends
164	13	W	Day increased 8h, 46m.
165	14	Th	Battle of Marengo 1800
166	15	F	Sun ris. 3,44.—sets 8, 16
167	16	S	D. of Marlborough d.1722
168	17	—	*2nd Sunday after Trinity*
169	18	M	Battle of Waterloo 1815
170	19	Tu	Magna Charta sign. 1215
171	20	W	Accession of Qn. Victoria
172	21	Th	Insurrection in Paris 1848
173	22	F	Sun ris. 3, 44.—sets 8, 18
174	23	S	Leibnitz born 1646 [Day
175	24	—	*3rd Sun. aft. Trin.* Mids.
176	25	M	Insur. quelled; 12,000 kd.
177	26	Tu	George IV.d.1830[&wnd.
178	27	W	Dr. Dodd executed 1777
179	28	Th	Q. Victoria crowned 1838
180	29	F	Rousseau born 1712
181	30	S	Day decreased 4 m.

Of every twenty shillings raised by taxation, half-a-crown only is required for the support of every branch of the civil government, while seventeen and sixpence goes to pay or provide for war.

During the 32 years of peace, our war establishments have cost us upwards of five hundred millions sterling.

The interest on the war debt, otherwise called the national debt, is for the present year, £28,045,000.

Since the peace in 1815, we have paid as interest on the national debt more than one thousand millions of money.

The annual cost of the civil government is but about six and a half millions sterling.

The Ancient Britons were noted for being swift of foot, having fine athletic frames, and great strength of body ; *their only drink was water.*

There is no virtue where there is no temptation. The man who throws down the glittering bait, who resists the tempter's guile, is the man who before heaven's tribunal will bear the test.—*Thomas Beggs.*

Not what I *have,* but what I *do* is my kingdom.—*Thos. Carlyle.*

How indistructibly the good grows and propagates itself, even among the weedy entanglements of evil.—*T. Carlyle.*

The poorest member of civilized society, who dedicates himself to profitable labour, is rich compared with the unproductive, and therefore, poor individuals of any civilized tribe.—*Charles Knight.*

It is the beautiful necessity of our nature to love something.—*Douglas Jerrold.*

What is man born for, but to be a reformer?—*R. W. Emerson.*

Whoso would be a man, must be a non-conformist.—*R. W. Emerson.*

A knave is a round about fool, a fool in circumbedibus.—*S. T.*

MONTHLY NOTICES.—*June 20th.* Overseers to fix on Church doors notice to persons qualified to vote for counties to make claims. Persons on the register need not make a new claim unless they have changed their qualification.

HINT TO MARRIED PEOPLE.—There is nothing that tends so much to keep the fire of love burning brightly as those little attentions which, *before* marriage, the two parties would consider themselves inexcusable in forgetting. This laying aside the little endearments that nursed love into being the very moment that you have solemnly vowed to live on it is almost perjury. Where people are joined for life, it is their mutual interest and duty to render themselves as interesting objects to one another as possible.

July.—31 days.

Full	.. .. 5th, 1h, 28m, afternoon
Last quarter..	13th, 7 7 morning
New	.. ..19th, 9 15 afternoon
First quarter,	27th, 0 35 morning

182	1	—	*4th Sunday after Trinity*
183	2	M	Cranmer born 1489
184	3	Tu	Dog Days begin
185	4	W	American Independ. 1776
186	5	Th	Sir T. More behd. 1535
187	6	F	Cambridge Term ends
188	7	S	Oxford Term ends
189	8	—	*5th Sunday after Trinity*
190	9	M	Sun ris. 3, 52.—sets 8, 12
191	10	Tu	Calvin born 1509
192	11	W	Day 16h, 12m, long
193	12	Th	Erasmus died 1536
194	13	F	Hunter born 1728
195	14	S	Bastile destroyed 1789
196	15	—	*6th Sun.aft. Trin*. St. Swi-
197	16	M	[thin's Day
198	17	Tu	Dr. Watts born 1674
199	18	W	Sun ris. 3, 59.—sets 8, 0
200	19	Th	Petrarch died 1374
201	20	F	Petrarch born 1304
202	21	S	Burns died 1796
203	22	—	*7th Sunday after Trinity*
204	23	M	Day breaks 18m, aft. mid.
205	24	Tu	Dr. Lardner died 1768
206	25	W	Romaine died 1795
207	26	Th	Day decreased 1h, 0m.
208	27	F	Revolution in Paris 1830
209	28	S	Cowley the Poet died 1667
210	29	—	*8th Sunday after Trinity*
211	30	M	Sun ris. 4, 16.—sets 7, 44
212	31	Tu	Gray the poet died 1771

ZIMMERMAN.—This ancient physician went from Hanover to attend Frederic the Great, in his last illness. One day the King said to him, " You have I presume, sir, sent many a man to another world." This was rather a bitter pill for the doctor; but the dose he gave the king in return was a judicious mixture of truth and flattery. " Not so many as your majesty, nor with so much honor to myself."

Let us ask, too, if the Bible is universally diffused in Hindostan, what must be the astonishment of the natives to find that we are forbidden to rob, murder, and steal; we who, in fifty years, have extended our empire from a few acres about Madras over the whole peninsula, and sixty millions of people; and examplified in our public conduct every crime of which human nature is capable. What matchless impudence to follow up such practice with such precepts! If we have common prudence let us keep the Gospel at home, and tell them that Machiavel is our prophet, and the god of the Manicheans our god.—*Rev. Sydney Smith.*

CLEAR DEFINITION.—Pray, Dr. Skruitz, what on airth is a horrorscope?" " Why, marm, you perceive that when the nocturnal hour is so far procrastinated by a superabundant application of the oleaginous, acidulous, piperine, mustardific, oviparous components of a crustæciopiscatory sallad, and its vinous and alcoholic accidents, an undue expansion of the stomachic integuments ensues, which is the progress of its constipating influences, stigmatises the cerebral functions, confuses the nervo-optic system, and gives a 'scope' to the ' horrors.' " " Lah ! '' Ladies of fashion starve their happiness to feed their vanity.

MONTHLY NOTICES.—*July 5th.* Annual Licenses to be taken out by Pawnbrokers and Appraisers. 20th. Poor's rates and assessed taxes due on the 6th of April last must be paid on or before this day by all Electors of cities or boroughs, or they will be disqualified from voting at an Election. Last day for sending in claims for counties. 30th. Overseers to make out lists of County and Borough Electors.

SEA SICKNESS.—The most effectual prevention is the horizontal position. Persons should put their stomach and bowels in proper order, by the use of mild aperients, before proceeding to sea.

August.—31 days.

MOON'S CHANGES.

Full .. .. 4th, 3h, 52m, morning
Last quarter, 11th, 1 32 afternoon
New .. .. 18th, 5 32 morning
First quarter, 25th, 4 55 afternoon

213	1	W	Lammas Day
214	2	Th	Gainsborough died, 1788
215	3	F	Arkwright died, 1792
216	4	S	Calais tkn. by Edward III
217	5	—	*9th Sunday after Trinity*
218	6	M	Oyster season commences
219	7	Tu	Sun ris. 4, 30—sets 7, 30
220	8	W	Canning died, 1827
221	9	Th	Dryden the poet b. 1631
222	10	F	Greenwich Obs. founded
223	11	S	Dog Days end [1675
524	12	—	*10th Sunday after Trinity*
225	13	M	Dow. Qn. Adelaide b. 1792
226	14	Tu	Printing invented, 1437
227	15	W	Length of day 14h, 35m
228	16	Th	Andrew Marvell d. 1678
229	17	F	Duchess of Kent b. 1786
230	18	S	Total ecl. of the sun invis
231	19	—	*11th Sunday after Trinity*
232	20	M	Blackcock shootg. begins
233	21	Tu	Day breaks at 2h, 33m.
234	22	W	Day decreased 2h, 19m.
235	23	Th	Wallace beheaded, 1305
236	24	F	[1770
237	25	S	Chatterton comm. suicide
238	26	—	*12th Sunday after Trinity*
239	27	M	Thomson the poet d. 1748
240	28	Tu	Sun ris. 5, 5—sets 6, 54
241	29	W	Locke born, 1632
242	30	Th	Dr. Paley born, 1743
243	31	F	John Bunyan died, 1688

We must punish crime without imitating it. The punishment of death is rarely anything but a useless barbarity.—*Catherine of Russia.*

It is said that Napoleon owed his death to the morbid state of his stomach, induced by snuff taking.

Of 1129 murders committed in France during the space of four years, 446 have been in consequence of quarrels and contentions in taverns. This tends to show the fatal influence of strong drinks.—*M. Quetilet.*

Whoso is heroic will always find crisis to try his edge. Human virtue demands her champions and martyrs ; and the tribe of persecution always proceeds.—*R. W. Emerson.*

Stir not up fire with the sword.—*Pythagoras.*

A loving heart is the beginning of all knowledge.—*Thos. Carlyle.*

For man's life, now as of old, is the genuine work of God ; wherever there is a man, a God is revealed, and all that is Godlike. A whole epitome of the infinite, with its meanings, lies unfolded in the life of one man.—*Thos. Carlyle*

The courage we desire and prize is not the courage to die decently, but to live manfully.—*Thomas Carlyle.*

Courtesy is the due of man to man, not of suit of clothes to suit of clothes.—*Thomas Carlyle.*

The highest and most ancient of all orders is that of manhood.—*Thomas Carlyle.*

The stout heart is also a warm and a kind one, affection dwells with danger, all the holier and the lovelier for such stern environment.—*Thomas Carlyle.*

Nature, when she does not mean us for mariners and vagabonds bids us stay at home.—*Charles Lamb.*

Nothing divine dies, all good is eternallyre-productive.—*R. W. Emerson.*

MONTHLY NOTICES.—*August 1st.* Annual Licenses to be taken out by Hawkers and Pedlars. The Two first Sundays County and Borough lists are to be affixed to the church doors. 20th. Last day for leaving with overseers objections to county electors. 25th. Last day for the service of objections to electors in counties, or their tenants ; and for service on overseers of objections to borough electors ; also the last day to claim as borough electors. 31st. All taxes and rates payable on March 1st. must be paid on or before this day by all persons claiming to be enrolled as burgesses.

The *Bolton Advertiser* is Published on the 1st of every month.

September,—30 days.

MOON'S CHANGES.
Full .. .. 2nd, 5h, 17m, afternoon
Last quarter, 9th, 6   55   „
New .. ..16th, 4   1   „
First quarter, 24th, 11 23   morning

244	1	S	Partridge Shooting begins
245	2	—	13th Sun. af. Trin. Eclip.
246	3	M	[of the Moon invisible
247	4	Tu	Sun ris. 5, 19.—sets 6, 38
248	5	W	Length of day 13h, 16m.
249	6	Th	Day decreased 3h, 18m.
250	7	F	Dr. Johnson born 1709
251	8	S	Ariosto born 1474
252	9	—	14th Sunday after Trinity
253	10	M	Wm. the Conqueror died
254	11	Tu	Thomson born 1700[1087
255	12	W	Day breaks 3h, 33m.
256	13	Th	Gen. Wolfe killed 1759
257	14	F	Moscow burnt 1812
258	15	S	Romaine born 1714
259	16	—	15th Sunday after Trinity
260	17	M	The year 5610 of the Jew-
261	18	Tu	[ish era commences
262	19	W	Battle of Poicters 1356
263	20	Th	Battle of Newbury 1643
264	21	F	Sun rises 5, 50.—sets 6, 1
265	22	S	Autumn commences
266	23	—	16th Sunday after Trinity
267	24	M	Equal day and night
268	25	Tu	Porson died 1808
269	26	W	Adm. Ld. Collingwood b.
270	27	Th	Brindley died 1772 [1748
271	28	F	Day decreased 4h, 50m.
272	29	S	MICHAELMAS DAY
273	30	—	17th Sunday after Trinity

A glutton may be crammed up to the throat with flesh meats, &c., but he can never be a diseased man unless he add spirituous or fermented liquors to his food.—*Dr. Darwin.*

In Hindostan none drink intoxicating draughts but the outcasts.—*Basil Montague.*

We do pray for mercy, and that same prayer should teach us all to render the deeds of mercy.—*Shakespear.*

I now no more think of drinking wine than a horse does. The wine upon the table is no more for me than for the dog under the table.—*Dr. Johnstone.*

Abstinence is better than temperance.—*Basil Montague.*

The Prince of Peace has an army of martyrs, but not of warriors.—*Brewin Grant.*

If the clock of the tongue be not set by the dial of the heart, it will not go right.

The god of battles is an heathen deity worshipped by professing christians.

Beer, wine, spirits, furnish no elements capable of entering into the composition of the blood, muscular fibre, or any part which is the seat of the vital principle.

There are only three ways to get out of a quarrel; write out, fight out, or back out; but the best way is to keep out.

Parents should not show unequal love for their children, as they make one proud, the other envious, and both fools.

Reason loses the race, if it sits in meditation on the fence, while competition rushes by.

Gilded roofs do not keep out sleepless nights.

A Christian profession saves many a good name in this life, but never a soul in the next.

Working men, let your sweat drops wash all dishonesty from your gains.

A bankruptcy of moral principles is the worst bankruptcy that can be imagined.

MONTHLY NOTICES.—*Sept. 5th.* Overseers to make out Burgess List and deliver to the Town Clerk. *8th.* Town Clerks to fix the "Burgess List" in some public place in the Borough from this day until the 15th. *15th.* Claims of persons omitted in the "Burgess List," and objections to persons improperly inserted therein, to be given to the Town Clerk, in writing, on or before this day; notice of objection to be also given to the person objected to. *24th.* List of claimants, and of persons objected to, to be fixed by the Town Clerk in some public place in each borough, from this day till 1st October. List of objections to county electors, and also claims and objections respecting borough lists, to be affixed to the church doors two Sundays preceding the 15th Sept.

October.—31 days.

Changes.
Full	..	.. 2nd, 5h, 33m, morning
Last quarter,	9th, 0	44 "
New	..16th, 5	13 "
First quarter,	24th, 7	3 "
Full	.:	..31st, 4 46 afternoon.

274	1	M	Lon. University op. 1828
275	2	Tu	Sun ris. 6, 10—sets 5,40
276	3	W	Tillotson born, 1730
277	4	Th	Rennie died, 1821
278	5	F	H. K. White died, 1806
279	6	S	Peace pr. with Amer. 1783
280	7	—	18th Sunday after Trinity
281	8	M	Length of day 11h, 5m.
282	9	Tu	[Term begins
283	10	W	Ox. Term begins. Cam.
284	11	Th	America discovered 1492
285	12	F	Day breaks 4h, 40m.
286	13	S	Canova the sculp. d. 1822
287	14	—	19th Sunday after Trinity
288	15	M	Sun ris. 6, 31—sets 5,15
289	16	Tu	Houses of Parliament bt.
290	17	W	Wilkes born 1727 [1834
291	18	Th	Day decreased 6h 3m.
292	19	F	Dean Swift died 1745
293	20	S	Sir C. Wren born 1632
294	21	—	20th Sunday after Trinity
295	22	M	Length of day 10h, 17m.
296	23	Tu	Battle of Edgehill 1642
297	24	W	Chaucer died 1400
298	25	Th	Battle of Agincourt 1415
299	26	F	Dr. Doddridge died 1751
300	27	S	Captain Cook born 1728
301	28	—	21st Sunday after Trinity
302	29	M	Sir W. Raleigh bhd. 1618
303	30	Tu	Sun ris. 7, 2—sets 4, 41
304	31	W	Allhallows Eve

The power of human life is the sole prerogative of him who gave it. Human laws, therefore, are in rebellion against this prerogative, when they transfer it to human hands.—*Dr. Rush.*

Industry and economy will get rich, while sagacity and intrigue are laying their plans.

A drone should be as rare in society as in a hive of bees, and almost deserves to be treated the same.

Trust him little who praises all, him less who censures all, and and him least who is indifferent about all.

VICE.—Though the gods should not know, and men should not punish, yet would I not commit it, so mean a thing is vice.—*Seneca.*

Read books, as bees, to fill your hive; and not as butterflies to paint your wings.—*Secker.*

The number of hospitals, infirmaries, and dispensaries in London is 150, one of which, in 1844, admitted 40,000 patients.

Witnesses are unwilling to testify and jurors to convict, where the sentence is death.

PRICES OF PROVISIONS FOUR CENTURIES AGO.—In 1471, the Wax Chandler's Company gave a public dinner, of which the following is a bill of fare, viz—two loins of mutton and two loins of veal, 2s. 4d.; a loin of beef, 4d.; a leg of mutton, 2d.; a pig, 4d.; a capon, 6d.; a coney, 2d.; a dozen of pigeons, 7d.; a hundred eggs, 8d; a goose, 6d.; jellies, 8d.; and a kilderkin of ale, 1s. 8d.—total, 7s. Plain and humble as the dinner was, it could not now be procured for less than £5.

I admire wit as I do wind : when it shakes the trees it is fine, when it cools the wave it is refreshing, when it steals over the flowers it is enchanting, but when it whistles through the key hole it is very unpleasant.—*Sir E. L. Bulwer.*

MONTHLY NOTICES.—Oct. 1st. Mayor and Assessors to hold an open court to revise the "Burgess List" sometime between the 1st and 15th of this month; three clear days notice of such court being given. The revised list to be kept by the Town Clerk. **10th.** Half-yearly dividend on various Stocks become due. **13th.** Fire Insurance due at Michaelmas must be paid on or before this day, or the policy becomes void. **15th.** Half-yearly dividend on old Three Per Cent Annuities becomes due.

Learn to respect the right of private judgement : what right hast thou to trample upon or treat with contempt thy brother's opinions.

November.—30 days.

MOON'S CHANGES.

Last quarter.. 7th, 8h, 22m, morning
New .. ..14th, 9 13 afternoon
First quarter, 23rd, 2 24 morning
Full .. ..30th, 3 25 ,,

305	1	Th	All Saints
306	2	F	Michaelmas T. begins
307	3	S	
308	4	—	*22nd Sunday after Trinity*
309	5	M	Gunpowder Plot
310	6	Tu	Princess Charlotte d. 1817
311	7	W	Sun ris. 7, 8—sets 4, 21
312	8	Th	Milton died 1674
313	9	F	Birth of Prince of Wales
314	10	S	Luther born 1483
315	11	—	*23rd Sunday after Trinity*
316	12	M	Cambridge Term divides
317	13	Tu	[at midnight
318	14	W	Bruce dis. scource of Nile
319	15	Th	Day decreased 7,42 [1770
320	16	F	Battle of Lutzen
321	17	S	Lord Erskine died 1823
322	18	—	*24th Sunday after Trinity*
323	19	M	Sun ris. 7, 30—sets 4, 8
324	20	Tu	
325	21	W	Princess Royal b. 1840
326	22	Th	St. Cecilia
327	23	F	Length of day 8h, 29m.
328	24	S	Peace with Amer. 1814
329	25	—	*25th Sunday after Trinity*
330	26	M	Michaelmas Term ends
331	27	Tu	Sun ris. 7, 45—sets 4, 2
332	28	W	Cardinal Wolsey d. 1530
333	29	Th	Oliver Goldsmith b. 1731
334	30	F	St. Andrew

BROTHER FARMERS,—I have watched the effects of teetotalism for more than two years, and have come to the conclusion that, instead of its being an injury to us, it would be an immense benefit.

I believe that in no way a working-man can spend his money, does it return with so little profit to the cultivator of the soil as when he lays it out in beer.

I only wish to call the attention of the agricultural world to the subject. As far as I have been able to ascertain, all those who have fairly examined the subject, are satisfied that the change that is now going on will be greatly to our advantage.

Suppose an individual to consume the very moderate quantity of one pint of beer per day; in the year it amounts, at twopence per pint, to £3. 0s. 10d.; with this amount of money, at different times in the course of the year, the teetotaler might purchase:

	£	s	d
29 lbs. of meat,	0	12	1
8 stone of good flour..	0	18	0
12 lbs. of butter, ...	0	12	0
3 sacks of potatoes, ..	0	12	0
6 stone of barleymeal,	0	6	9
	£3	0	10

		s.	d.
Take off profit to the butcher		1	3
Do. to the Baker,		2	7
		0 3	10

And a net sum of £2 17 0 is left to the farmer for the produce of the soil. When this sum is expended for beer, how stands the profit to the farmer?

" To make 365 pints of twopenny beer, about five bushels of barley are required; this is purchased of the farmer for 16s. 8d., and that is all he receives of the money; the remaining £2 4s. 2d. goes to the Queen's

(Dec. page.)

MONTHLY NOTICES.—*Nov. 1st.* Borough Councillors to be elected. **9th.** Mayor and Aldermen of boroughs to be elected. **15th.** Attornies and others to take out Certificates.

THREE BAD HABITS—beware of them. 1st. Giving way to the ease and indulgence of the moment, instead of doing what ought to be done. 2nd. When making a good resolution and partially failing in its accomplishment, to abandon it altogether. 3rd. The practice of eating and drinking things because they are on the table, especially when they are injurious, or have to be paid for.

Moon's Changes.

Last quarter, 6th, 6h, 52m, afternoon
New   .. ..14th, 3 37   "
First quarter, 22nd, 7 40   "
Full   .. ..29th, 2 0   "

335	1	S	Buonaparte crowned 1804
336	2	—	*Advent Sunday*
337	3	M	James II, abdicated 1688
338	4	Tu	Sun ris. 7, 53.—sets 3, 59
339	5	W	Day decreased 8h, 34m.
340	6	Th	Daybreak 5h, 56.
341	7	F	Algernon Sydney behead
342	8	S	Milton born 1608 [1683
343	9	—	*2nd Sunday in Advent*
344	10	M	Length of day 7h, 56m.
345	11	Tu	Gay the poet died 1732
346	12	W	Colley Cibber died 1757
347	13	Th	Dr. Johnson died 1781
348	14	F	Daybreak 6h. 0m.
349	15	S	Izaak Walton died 1683
350	16	—	*3rd Sunday in Advent*
351	17	M	Oxford Term ends
352	18	Tu	Sun ris. 8, 3.—sets 3, 52
353	19	W	Ember Week
354	20	Th	Gray the poet born 1716
355	21	F	Shortest Day
356	22	S	Wollaston died 1828
357	23	—	*4th Sunday in Advent*
358	24	M	Daybreak 6h. 1m.
359	25	Tu	CHRISTMAS DAY
360	26	W	St. Stephen
361	27	Th	St. John
362	28	F	Innocent's Day
363	29	S	Sun rises 8, 7.—sets 4, 0.
364	30	—	*1st Sunday after Christmas*
365	31	M	Day increased 4m.

duty, for labour, licenses, and profit to the brewer and distiller, and retailer.
Under the teetotal system the farmer receives out of
£3 0 10 ....£2 17 0
Under the Drinkg. system 0 16 8

Leaving a balance of 2 0 4 in favour of agriculture, by carrying out universal sobriety."
Here are plain facts and figures ! Let the farmer and his labourer carefully examine them before he again inquires, What is to become of the barley ?
A FARMER.—
(From the Economist.)

READING PRAYERS.—The old King (Frederick Wm.), had a strong sense of religion, though he expressed it at times with a vehemence truly comic. Being too unwell to read the usual prayers himself, his daily practice, he desired his valet de chambre to read them to him. His attendant thinking it disrespectful to *thou* a King, on coming to the words " The Lord bless thee," changed the expression into " The Lord bless you."—" It is not so, read it again," cried the exasperated King, at the same time throwing something at the reader's head. The poor fellow could not conceive what blunder he had made, and again read "The Lord bless *you*." The king was furious, and having nothing else at hand he pulled off his nightcap and flung it in the attendant's face, crying " It is not so, I tell you read it again." The frightened valet again gasped fourth in scarcely audible accents, " The Lord bless *you*."— " Bless *thee*, rogue," roared the Monarch, losing all patience and self-control, " bless *thee*." Dont you know, fellow, that in the sight of God I am only a miserable rascal like yourself ?— *Campbell's, Frederick the Great*

MONTHLY NOTICES.—Dec 31st. Those who have not been accustomed to keep an account of personal or household expenses, should begin from this day. Those in trade who have not been accustomed to take an annnal account of stock, should begin from this day. Without cash-books, and without stock-books, trade is little better than a game of chance.

I make not my head a grave, but a treasury of knowledge ; I intend no monopoly, but a community of learning ; I study not for my own sake, but theirs who study not for themselves : I envy no man that knows more than myself, but I pity him that knows less.— *Sir Thomas Brown.*

The *Bolton Advertiser* is Published on the 1st of every month.

The Royal Family.

QUEEN VICTORIA, (only child of Edward, Duke of Kent; who was born Nov. 2, 1767, and died January 23, 1820,) *born* May 24, 1819, *suc.* June 20, 1837, *cr.* June 28, 1838, *mar.* Feb. 10, 1840, to

FRANCIS ALBERT AUGUSTUS CHARLES EMANUEL, Duke of Saxe, Prince of Coburg and Gotha, *born* August 26, 1819.

Issue—VICTORIA ADELAIDE MARY LOUISA, *Pncs. Royal, b.* Nov. 21; 1840.
ALBERT EDWARD, *Prince of Wales, b.* Nov. 9, 1841.
ALICE MAUD MARY, *b.* April 15, 1843.—ALFRED ERNEST ALBERT, *b.* Augt. 6, 1844.
HELENA AUGUSTA, *b.* May 25, 1846.—LOUISA CAROLINA ALBERTA, *b.* Mar. 18, 1848.

	BORN.		BORN.
King of Hanover	June 5, 1771	Duchess of Kent	Aug. 17, 1786
Dowager Queen Adelaide	Aug. 13, 1792	Duchess of Cambridge	Mar. 25, 1797
Duke of Cambridge	Feb. 24, 1774	Crown Prince of Hanover	May 27, 1817
Duchess of Gloucester	Apl. 25, 1776	Prince George of Cambridge	Mar. 26, 1819
Princess Sophia	Nov. 3, 1777	Pncs. Augusta of Cambridge	Juiy 19, 1822
Princess Sophia Matilda	May 23, 1773	Princess Mary of Cambridge	Nov. 27, 1833

Her Majesty's Ministers of the Cabinet.

First Lord of the Treasury (Premier)	Lord John Russell
Lord Chancellor	Lord Cottenham
Lord President of the Council	The Marquis of Lansdown
Lord Privy Seal	The Earl of Minto
Secretaries of State.. { Home	Sir George Grey
Foreign	Lord Palmerston
Colonial	Earl Grey
Chancellor of the Exchequer	The Right Hon. Charles Wood
President of the Board of Control	Sir J. C. Hobhouse
President of the Board of Trade	Right Hon. H. Labouchere
First Lord of the Admiralty	The Earl of Auckland
Paymaster-General	The Right Hon. T. B. Macaulay
Chancellor of the Duchy of Lancaster	Lord Campbell
Chief Commissioner of Woods & Forests,	Earl of Carlisle
Postmaster-General	The Marquis of Clanricarde

MINISTERS NOT OF THE CABINET.

Commander-in-Chief	The Duke of Wellington
Master-General of the Ordnance	The Marquis of Anglesey
Vice-President of the Board of Trade,	Earl Granville
Master of the Mint	The Right Hon. Richard Lalor Sheil
Secretary-at-War	The Right Hon. Fox Maule
Secretary of the Admiralty	H. G. Ward, Esq.
Secretaries of the Treasury	J. Parker, Esq., H. Tufnell, Esq.
Secretaries of the Board of Control..	The Right Hon. G. S. Byng, T. Wyse, Esq.
Under Secretaries.. { Home	S. M. Philips, Esq., Sir D. Le Merchant
Foreign	Rt. Hon. E. J. Stanley, H. Addington, Esq.
Colonial	B. Hawes, Esq., J. Stephen, Esq.
Lords of the Treasury	{ Right Hon. Sir Chas. Wood, Bart., Vicount Ebrington, H. Rich, W. G. Craig, Esqrs.
Lords of the Admiralty	{ Admiral J. W. D. Dundas, Rear-Admiral H. Prescott, Capt. the Hon. F. Berkeley, Capt. Lord J. Hay, the Hon. W. F. Cowper.
Ordnance .. { Secretary	Lord Charles Paget
Clerk	Lieutenant-Colonel the Hon. G. Anson
Surveyor-General	Major-General C. R. Fox
Attorney-General	Sir John Jervis
Solicitor-General	Sir John Romiley, Q. C.
Judge-Advocate	

IRELAND.

Lord-Lieutenant.. The Earl of Clarendon
Lord Chancellor.. The Rt. Hon. M. Brady
Chief Secretary .. Sir William Somerville
Attorney-General, Jas. H. Monaghan, Esq.
Solicitor-General,

SCOTLAND.

Ld. High Constable, The Earl of Errol
Ld. Privy Seal...... Viscount Melville
Ld. Advocate...... Rt. Hon. A. Rutherford
Solicitor-General.. T. Maitland, Esq.
Chief Justice...... The Hon. David Bayle

15

Commercial and other Stamps.

RECEIPTS.

£		£	s.	d.
If 5 .. .. .. and under		10 ..	0	3
10 .. .. .. —		20 ..	0	6
20 .. .. .. —		50 ..	1	0
50 .. .. .. —		100 ..	1	6
100 .. .. .. —		200 ..	2	6
200 .. .. .. —		300 ..	4	0
300 .. .. .. —		500 ..	5	0
500 .. .. .. —		1000 ..	7	6
1000 .. .. and upwards		..	10	0
Receipts in full for all demands		..	10	0

N.B. Receipt stamps not necessary if money be paid by promissory notes, &c., provided the receipt be written on the back of the note.

Persons receiving the money are compellable to pay the duty.

BILLS AND PROMISSORY NOTES.

Not exceeding two months after date, or sixty days after sight. / For a longer period.

£ s.		£ s.	s. d.	s. d.
If.... 2 0		5 5	1 0	1 6
Above 5 5		20 0	1 6	2 0
— 20 0	not exceeding	30 0	2 0	2 6
— 30 0		50 0	2 6	3 6
— 50 0		100 0	3 6	4 6
— 100 0		200 0	4 6	5 0
— 200 0		300 0	5 0	6 0
— 300 0		500 0	6 0	8 0
— 500 0	and	1000 0	8 6	12 6
— 1000 0		2000 0	12 6	15 0

N.B. Promissory notes on demand made out of Great Britain, shall not be negotiable in Great Britain, whether they are payable in Great Britain or not, unless they have the above duties.

Penalty for post-dating Bills of Exchange £100.

FOREIGN BILLS OF EXCHANGE, IN SETS.

For every Bill of each Set

£		£	s.	d.
Not exceeding..		100 ..	1	0
Above 100 .. —		200 ..	3	0
— 200 .. —		500 ..	4	0
— 500 .. —		1000 ..	5	0
— 1000 .. —		2000 ..	7	6
— 2000 .. —		3000 ..	10	6
— 3000		..	15	0

BONDS AND MORTGAGES.

		£	s.	
Not exceeding £50		1	0	
£50 and not exceeding £100 ..		1	10	
100 —		200 ..	2	0
200 —		300 ..	3	0
300 —		500 ..	4	0
500 —		1000 ..	5	0
1000 —		2000 ..	6	0
2000 —		3000 ..	7	0
3000 —		4000 ..	8	0
4000 —		5000 ..	9	0
5000 —		10000 ..	12	0

APPRENTICES' INDENTURES.

		£	£ s.	
When the premium is under		30 ..	1 0	
If £30 .. .. and under		50 ..	2 0	
50 .. .. —		100 ..	3 0	
100 .. .. —		200 ..	6 0	
200 .. .. —		300 ..12 0		
300 .. .. —		400 ..20 0		
400 .. .. —		500 ..25 0		

If no premium, £1; or £1 15s. if more than 1,080 words.—Indentures of apprentices for the sea-service exempt.

CONVEYANCES.

		£	£	s.
Where Purchase Money shall not amount to		20 ..	0	10
Shall amount to				
£20 and not amount to		50 ..	1	0
50 —		150 ..	1	10
150 —		300 ..	2	0
300 —		500 ..	3	0

and so on up to £100,000.

PROBATES OF WILLS AND LETTERS OF ADMINISTRATION.

			With a Will.	Without a Will.
		£	£ s.	£ s.
Above the value of £20 and under 50			......	0 10
If 20 —		100	0 10	......
50 —		100	......	1 0
100 —		200	2 0	3 0
200 —		300	5 0	8 0
300 —		450	8 0	11 0
450 —		600	11 0	15 0
600 —		800	15 0	22 0
800 —		1000	22 0	30 0
1000 —		1500	30 0	45 0
1500 —		2000	40 0	60 0
2000 —		3000	50 0	75 0
3000 —		4000	60 0	90 0
4000 —		5000	80 0	120 0
5000 —		6000	100 0	150 0
6000 —		7000	120 0	180 0
7000 —		8000	140 0	210 0
8000 —		9000	160 0	240 0
9000 —		10000	180 0	270 0
10000 —		12000	200 0	300 0

The scale continues to increase up to £1,000,000.

AGREEMENTS.

Of the value of £200 and upwards, containing only 1,080 words, £1; more than 1,080 words, £1 15s; and for every further 1,080 words, £1 5s.

LEASE FOR A YEAR.

			£	s.
When Purchase Money shall not amount to £20.			0	10
Shall amount to £20, and not amount to £50.			0	15
ditto £50.. .. £150..			1	0
ditto £150. or upwards			1	15

DUTIES ON LEGACIES.—Of the value of £20, or upwards, out of Personal Estate, or charged upon Real Estate, &c.; and upon every share of residue :—To a child or parent, or any lineal descendant or ancestor of the deceased, £1 per cent. To a brother or sister, or their descendants, £3 per cent. To an uncle or aunt, or their descendants, £5 per cent. To a great uncle or great aunt, or their decendants, £6 per cent. To any other relation, or any stranger in blood, £10 per cent. Legacy to husband or wife, exempt. If the deceased died prior to the 5th April, 1805, the duty only attaches on personal estates, and by a lower scale.

LICENSES.

For Marriage, if special £5	0	For Appraisers £0	16
Ditto, if not special..	0	10	For Hawkers and Pedlars, on foot . 4	0
For Bankers 30	0	Ditto, with one horse, ass, or mule 8	0
For Pawnbrokers within the limits		Selling Beer, to be drunk on the	
of the twopenny post.. 15	0	premises 3	3
Elsewhere 7	10	Do. not to be drunk on the premises 1	1

𝔄𝔰𝔰𝔢𝔰𝔰𝔢𝔡 𝔗𝔞𝔵𝔢𝔰.

WINDOW TAX.

Win-dows.	Duty per Annum.			Win-dows.	Duty per Annum.			Win-dows.	Duty per Annum.			Win-dows.	Duty per Annum.		
	£	s.	d.		£	s.	d.		£	s.	d.		£	s.	d.
8	0	16	6	16	3	18	6	24	7	5	9	32	10	13	3
9	1	1	0	17	4	7	0	25	7	14	3	33	11	1	6
10	1	8	0	18	4	15	3	26	8	2	9	34	11	10	0
11	1	16	3	19	5	3	9	27	8	11	0	35	11	18	3
12	2	4	9	20	5	12	3	28	8	19	6	36	12	6	9
13	2	13	3	21	6	0	6	29	9	8	0	37	12	15	3
14	3	1	9	22	6	9	0	30	9	16	3	38	13	3	6
15	3	10	0	23	6	17	6	31	10	4	9	39	13	12	0

Farm-houses belonging to Farms under £200 a-year are exempt.

MALE SERVANTS.

No.	Each Servant.			No.	Each Servant.			No.	Each Servant.		
	£	s.	d.		£	s.	d.		£	s.	d.
1	1	4	0	5	2	9	0	9	3	1	0
2	1	11	0	6	2	11	6	10	3	6	6
3	1	18	0	7	2	12	6	11	3	16	6
4	2	3	0	8	2	16	0				

HORSES.—For Riding or Drawing Carriages.

No.	Each Horse.	No.	Each Horse.	No.	Each Horse.
1	£1 8 9	5	£2 15 9	9	£3 0 9
2	2 7 3	6	2 18 0	10	3 3 6
3	2 12 3	7	2 19 9	11	3 3 6
4	2 15 6	8	2 19 9	12	3 3 6

₊ By cap. 17, 3 & 4 Vict., an additional £10 per cent. is imposed upon all the Assessed Taxes, Customs, and Excise.

WEATHER TABLE,

Constructed by Dr. HERSCHELL, and Improved by Dr. ADAM CLARKE.
The result of many years' actual observation, and is so near the truth that it will rarely be found to fail.

·Moon. Time of change.	In Summer.	In Winter.
Between midnight and 2 in the morning.... }	Fair {	Hard frost, unless wind be s. or s. w.
— 2 and 4 morning..	Cold, with frequent showers	Snow and stormy
— 4 - 6 — ..	Rain ..	Rain
— 6 - 8 — ..	Wind and rain ..	Stormy
— 8 - 10 — ..	Changeable ..	C. rain, if wind w. Snow if E.
— 10 - 12 — ..	Frequent showers	Cold and high wind
At 12 at noon, and to 2,p.m.	Very rainy	Snow or rain
Between 2 and 4 aftern. ..	Changeable ..	Fair and mild
— 4 - 6 — ..	Fair ..	Fair
— 6 - 8 — {	Fair, if wind N.W. rainy } if s. or s. w.	Fair & frosty if wind N. or N. E. Rain or snow if s. or s.
— 8 - 10 — ..	Ditto ..	Ditto [w.
— 10 and midnight ..	Fair	Fair and frosty

The nearer the time of the Moon's change, First quarter, Full, and Last quarter, is to *Midnight*, the fairer will the weather be during the seven days following. The nearer to *Mid-day* or *Noon* these phases of the Moon happen, the more foul or wet the weather may be expected during the next seven days.

17

Bolton Poor Law Union.

POPULATION of the Union, which comprises an area of 40,955 statute acres, taken in June, 1841 : Males, 48,350 ; Females, 49,169 ; Total, 97,519.

Total number of inhabited houses in June, 1841 : 18,029; uninhabited, 2,268.

Population of the Parish of Bolton, June, 1841—73,898
Do.　　　　do.　　　Deane.　　do.　　　26,217
Do.　　　　do.　　　Farnworth,do.　　　4,829

CLERK TO THE UNION, John Woodhouse, Solicitor, Acres'-field.

AUDITOR for the District, of which Bolton Union forms part, C. Mott, Esq., Ardwick-place, Stockport Road, Manchester.

BOARD OF GUARDIANS.

Population

33,609 *Great Bolton*..Dan Wood Latham, John Dean, Isaac Barrow, Richard Dunderdale, and James Cooper

16,144 *Little Bolton*..James Wardle ,Richard Nightingale, and John Entwisle

827 *Bradshaw*..John Hamer

1,309 *Breightmet*..Henry Holt

1,697 *Edgeworth*..James Walsh

555 *Entwisle*..John Ashworth, junr.

4,820 *Farnworth*..James Longworth

3,245 *Halliwell*..John Nuttall

1,996 *Harwood*..Charles Hopwood

713 *Heaton*..John Green

3,774 *Horwich*..Henry Hibbert

3,052 *LittleHulton*..Thos.Hodson

Population

902 *Middle Hulton*..John Cunliffe

445 *Over Hulton*..Hugh Stirrup

3,435 *Kersley*..John Tickle

1,701 *Darcy Lever*..Thos. Brown

657 *Great Lever*..George Piggot

2,580 *Little Lever*..Samuel Heys

149 *Longworth*..Wm. Holden

625 *Lostock*..Ralph Shaw

370 *Quarlton*..James Winder

Rumworth..James Marsh

2879 *Sharples*..Nathaniel Greenhalgh

2,627 *Tonge-with-Haulgh*..Thos. Holden

3,517 *Turton*..John Ashworth, senr.

4,527 *Westhoughton*..James Sylvester and Peter Ditchfield

EX-OFFICIO GUARDIANS.

The County Magistrates acting for the division of Bolton, for which see list.

Board Room, Acres'-field. Meetings, every Wednesday, at 9, a.m.

OVERSEERS.

Great Bolton..John Harwood, W. Hargreaves, Thomas Wood Heaton, and James Taylor

Little Bolton..James Marsden and George Binks

Halliwell..Thomas Cross, James Ormrod, and John Nuttall

Longworth..John Walmsley and Thomas Simm

Sharples..Joseph Thwaites, Robt. Orrell, sen., and John Mangnall

Turton..John Ashworth, sen.,John Knowles, and William Horrocks

Farnworth..Samuel Tonge, James Longworth, and David Edwards

Little Hulton..William Hilton, Thos. Higson, and Thos. Hodson

Rumworth..William Green and Richard Marsh

Bradshaw..John Hamer and Saml. Scowcroft

Breightmet..John Heaton and Jno. Seddon

Darcy Lever..George Smith and Robert Norris

Edgeworth..Jno.Brandwood,Thos. Bentley, and William Entwisle

Entwisle..Thomas Briggs and Jas. Mather

Harwood..Charles Hopwood, Jcb. Warburton, and James Fletcher

Quarlton..George Millington and John Seddon

18

Middle Hulton..John Cunliffe and Giles Seddon

Over Hulton..Hugh Stirrup and Joseph Hampson

Kersley..John Tickle and John Partington

Great Lever..Joseph Heys and Peter Johnson

Little Lever..RichardRadcliffe and John Bromiley

Tonge-with-Haulgh..Jno. Leyland, Joseph Phethean, Thos. Holden, John Gray, and John Bleakley

Heaton..John Lowe & Thos. Lee

Horwich..Wlliam Longworth and William Bennett, senr.

Westhoughton..James Higson and Robert Walker

Lostock..Ralph Shaw and Richard Latham

DISTRICT COLLECTORS.

Great Bolton..Jno.Seddon Scowcroft, Assistant Overseer, Office, Folds street, Great Bolton ; Thomas Balshaw, Thomas Platt, and James Wardle, Collectors.

Little Bolton District : comprising Little Bolton, Halliwell, Longworth, Sharples, and Turton—Thos. Dawson, office, Town Hall, Little Bolton.

Farnworth District : comprising Farnworth, Kersley, and Little Lever, —John Smith, office, High Style Fold, Kersley.

Hulton District : comprising Little Hulton, Middle Hulton, Over Hulton, and Rumworth—Thos. Fearnhead, office, Daubhill, Rumworth.

Lever District : comprising Bradshaw, Breightmet, Darcy Lever, Edgeworth, Entwisle, Harwood, Quarlton,and Tonge-with-Haulgh.—Robt. Makant, office, Barn-street, Little Bolton.

Westhoughton District : comprising Heaton, Horwich, Westhoughton, and Lostock—James Cooper, Westhoughton.

RELIEVING OFFICERS AND MEDICAL OFFICERS.

Bolton Eastern District : John Bradshaw, Bridgeman-place, Great Bolton. Surgeon and Vaccinator, Richard Snape, Dispensary Buildings, Great Bolton.

Bolton Central District : David Crossley, Bridgeman-place, Gt. Bolton

Bolton Western District : John Scowcroft Nelson, Cannon street, Great Bolton. Surgeon and Vaccinator, Joseph Denham, Bridge street, Great Bolton.

Little Bolton District : John Kenyon, Higher Bridge street, Little Bolton. Surgeon and Vaccinator, Jas. Pendlebury, Bridge street, Little Bolton.

Hulton and Farnworth Districts : Peter Thornley, Kersley. Surgeon and Vaccinator, G. L. Anderton, Halshaw Moor.

Lever District : Edward Greenhalgh, All Saint's street, Little Bolton. Surgeon and Vaccinator, Thos. Blackledge Garstang, Bark street, Little Bolton.

Westhoughton District : James Hodkinson, Westhoughton. Surgeon and Vaccinator, Frederick William Marshall, Horwich.

MASTERS OF THE UNION WORKHOUSES.

Job Harrison, *BoltonWorkhouse*, Fletcher-street, Great Bolton. Robt. Lowe, *Turton Workhouse*, Turton.

Registrars of Marriages.

Superintendent Registrar, John Woodhouse, Solicitor, Acres'-field.

Jas. Mather, Pilkington-st., Great Bolton

R. Prestwich,Greenside,Farnworth

David Nimmo, Bath-street, Little Bolton

John Hall, Ridgway Gates

Thos. Kenyon, Commission street, Great Bolton

Stephen Rothwell, Turton street, Little Bolton

BUILDINGS LICENSED FOR MARRIAGES IN THE UNION.

Catholic Chapel, Pilkington-street, Great Bolton.

Independent Chapel, Halshaw Moor, Farnworth.

Independent Meeting House, Mawdsley-street, Great Bolton.

The Presbyterian Chapel of the Unitarian Denomination, Bank-street, Great Bolton.

Duke's-Alley Chapel, Duke's-Alley Great Bolton.

Unitarian Meeting House, Moor-lane, Great Bolton.

Independent Methodist Chapel, Folds-road, Little Bolton.

The New Jerusalem Church, Halshaw Moor, Kersley.

The Wesleyan Methodist Chapel, Higher Bridge-street, Little Bolton.

The Baptist Chapel, Moor-lane, Gt. Bolton.

Registrars of Births and Deaths in the Union.

Superintendent Registrar, John Woodhouse, Solicitor, Acres'-field; Office hours, from ten till four

Bolton Eastern District: comprising part of the Township of Great Bolton; John Seddon Scowcroft, Bridgman street.

Bolton Western District: (remaining part of the Township of Great Bolton); Thomas Balshaw, Derby street

Little Bolton: comprising the whole township, except the higher end or detached part thereof; Thomas Dawson, Chapel street.

Sharples District: comprising the higher end of Little Bolton and Sharples; Robert Knowles, Astley Bridge, Sharples.

Halliwell District: comprising Halliwell and Heaton; Wm. Makant.

Westhoughton District: Township of Westhoughton; James Partington, senr., Schoolmaster, Westhougthon.

Farnworth District: comprising Farnworth and Kersley; Samuel Tonge, New Bury, Farnworth.

Lever District: comprising Darcy Lever, Great Lever, and Little Lever; Andrew Nelson, View Tree, Darcy Lever.

Tonge-with-Haulgh District: comprising Tonge-with-Haulgh, Breightmet & Harwood; Rt. Horrobin, Damside bridge, Tonge-with-Haulgh

Horwich District: comprising Horwich and Lostock; Wm. Thorp, Horwich.

Hulton District: comprising Little Hulton, Middle Hulton, Over Hulton, and Rumworth; John Eckersley, Daubhill, Rumworth.

Edgeworth District: comprising Edgeworth, Entwisle, and Quarlton; James Barnes, Moorside, Farmer, Edgeworth.

Turton District: comprising Bradshaw, Longworth, and Turton; Peter Haslam, Birtenshaw, Turton.

COUNTY MAGISTRATES ACTING FOR THIS DIVISION.

Robert Lomax, Esq.
John Fletcher, Esq.
William Ford Hulton, Esq.
Robert Heywood, Esq.
Robert Andrews, Esq.
Peter Ainsworth, Esq.
Henry Ashworth, Esq.
James Rothwell Barnes, Esq.
John Shepherd Birley, Clerk.

Charles James Darbyshire, Esq.
James Kay, Esq.
Joseph Ridgway, Esq.
John Hargreaves, jun., Esq.
James Hardcastle, Esq.
Peter Rothwell, Esq.
Peter Ormrod, Esq.
Edmund Ashworth, Esq.

CORPORATION.
BOROUGH MAGISTRATES.

Thomas Lever Rushton, Esq., Mayor
Thomas Cullen, Esq.
Robert Walsh, Esq.
Edmund Ashworth, Esq.
James Arrowsmith, Esq.

Thomas Thomasson, Esq.
Stephen Blair, Esq., M.P.
Ridgway Bridson, Esq.
William Ford Hulton, Esq.
James Knowles, Esq.

20

MUNICIPAL OFFICERS.

MAYOR—THOMAS LEVER RUSHTON, Esq.

Town Clerk—James Knowles, Esq.

Clerk to the Magistrates--James Winder, Esq.

Recorder –R. B. Armstrong, Esq.

Clerk of the Peace—J. Gordon, Esq.

Coroner—John Taylor, Esq.

Borough Prosecutor—J. Gaskell, Esq.

Treasurer—J. R. Wolfenden, Esq.

Superint. of the Market—J. Fogg.

Superint. of Police—James Harris.

Inspector of Weights and Measures —James Fogg.

Billet Master—James Harris.

Inspector of Hawkers' Licenses— James Harris.

Man. of Waterworks---T. Green

Inspector of Nuisances, James Fogg

TOWN COUNCIL.

EXCHANGE WARD.—Aldermen, Thomas Parkinson and William Cannon. Councillors, Thomas Cross, John Pilkington, Edward Bolling, Roger Hampson, Robert Moscrop and Thomas Lever Rushton, Mayor.

BRADFORD WARD—Aldermen, James Hargreaves and William Walker. Councillors, Joseph|Heys, Thomas Ormrod, John Hick, Wm. Henry Wright, Alexander Whowell, and Dan Wood Latham.

DERBY WARD.—Aldermen, James Scowcroft and James Eckersley. Councillors, Thomas Chantler, James Walsh, Peter Rothwell, John Knight, James Ormrod, and John Young.

CHURCH WARD.—Aldermen, William Gray, and George Piggot. Councillors, Thomas Myerscough, John Scowcroft, John Johnson, Johnson Lomax, Jonathan Warr, and John Barrow.

EAST WARD.—Aldermen, Robert Burton and Richard Crompton. Councillors, George Binks, John Lomax, Thomas Thomasson, Joseph Ainsworth, John Entwisle, and Robert Crook.

WEST WARD.---Aldermen, Richard Cooper and James Greenroyd. Councillors, Giles Cross, George Wolstenholme, Thomas Cocksey, William Ryder, Robert Knowles, and John Stones.

☞ The first named Alderman for each Ward has five years to serve; the second, two years. The two first Councillors in each Ward have three years to serve; the second two, two years; and the last two, one year.

QUARTERLY MEETINGS:—The second Wednesdays in February, May, and August, and the 9th of November; to be holden at Ten o'clock in the first three instances, and at twelve o'clock on November 9th.

ALDERMEN TO PRESIDE AT ELECTIONS.—Exchange Ward, Mr. Parkinson; Bradford Ward, Mr. Hargreaves; Derby Ward, Mr. Scowcroft; Church Ward, Mr. Gray; East Ward, Mr. Burton; West Ward, Mr. Greenroyd.

APPOINTMENT OF COMMITTEES.—Watch : The Mayor; Aldermen Greenroyd, Walker, Parkinson, Eckersley, James Scowcroft; Councillors Johnson, Young, Entwisle, Knowles, Wright, Barrow, Cocksey, Binks, Thomas Ormrod, Walsh, John Scowcroft, and Moscrop.

Fire Police : The Mayor; Aldermen Eckersley, Parkinson; Councillors Johnson Lomax, Ryder, Warr, Knight, Latham, Stones, Giles Cross, and Moscrop.

Waterworks . The Mayor; Aldermen Scowcroft, Piggot, Walker, Cooper, Greenroyd, Burton; Councillors Knight, Thomas Cross, Wolstenholme, Cocksey, Myerscough, Thomasson, Giles Cross and Walsh.

Finance: The Mayor; Aldermen Burton, Scowcroft, Hargreaves, Gray, Cannon; Councillors Stones, Hick, James Ormrod, Moscrop, Ainsworth, Myerscough, and Thomas Cross.

Sanitary: The Mayor; Aldermen Grey, Piggot; Councillors Wolstenholme, Pilkington, Hick, Thomas Cross, Whowell, Giles Cross, Rothwell, Barrow, Wright, Chantler, James Ormrod and Myerscough.

Remission of Borough Rates.—The Mayor; Alderman Burton; Councillors Stones, Hampson, Binks, Ainsworth, Johnson Lomax, Ryder & Crook.

General Purposes.—The Mayor; Alderman Cannon; Councillors Bolling, Ainsworth, Hampson, Whowell and Johnson.

County Court—Town Hall, Little Bolton.

Judge—W. A. Hulton, Esq., Barrister-at-Law.

Clerk—Thomas Holden, Solicitor, Acres'-field.

Treasurer—George Park, Esq., Liverpool.

High-Bailiffs—William Lomax, Exchange-street East; and John Lomax, Acres'-field. Meets every alternate Friday, at nine o'clock.

BOLTON POST OFFICE, BRADSHAWGATE.

The following statement exhibits the time of Arrival and Departure of the various Mails:—

Departures.

Time of closing,	For what Mail closed,	Time of despatch,
9 5. a.m.	Manchester, Birmingham, Leeds, S. Wales, &c.; Liverpool, Ireland, N. Wales, &c.	9 20 a.m.
12 35 p.m.	Manchester, Liverpool, Ireland, the North, Preston, Wigan, &c.	12 45 p.m.
5 30 p.m.	London, Oxford, Falmouth, Exeter, &c.; Liverpool, Birmingham, Manchester, Leeds, S. Wales, &c.	6 15 p.m.
9 45 p.m.	London. Wigan, and general North. Liverpool. Manchester, &c.	10 15 p.m.

On Sundays.

5 30 p.m.	London, &c. Liverpool, &c. Wigan, &c. Manchester.	6 0 p.m.
8 45 p.m.	Liverpool, &c. Manchester (direct).....	9 0 p.m.

Arrivals.

Time of Arrival.	Where from.
6 30 a.m.	Wigan and general North. London, &c. Liverpool, Ireland. Manchester, &c.
8 45 a.m.	Manchester, &c., including Preston, and North Letters posted late the preceding evening.
2 30 p.m.	Manchester, &c.
7 5 p.m	London, &c. Liverpool. Manchester, &c.

On Sundays.

6 30 a.m.	Manchester. London &c. Liverpool. Wigan &c.
8 15 a.m.	Manchester, &c.
6 45 p.m.	Liverpool, &c. Manchester.

Letters can be forwarded on payment of the revenue late fee, until five minutes before the time of despatch.

The boxes at the receiving houses in Great and Little Bolton, are closed, daily, at *ten minutes to five o'clock*, afternoon, for the London, Manchester, Birmingham, Leeds, and general South mails, and the bags are taken by the letter carriers of each district to the office in Bradshawgate, at five o'clock; of course, after that time letters intended for the above mails may, from five to half-past five, be posted at the chief office and pass without extra charge and from half-past 5 to ten minutes to 6, at the same place, on payment of the revenue late fee. The boxes of the local receiving houses are again closed for the second London, Liverpool, and South and North mails, *at nine o'clock, evening ;* letters for the same mails may be posted afterwards, at the chief office, in Bradshawgate, up to a quarter to ten o'clock, without fee, and on payment of the prescribed fee up to ten minutes past ten. The fee it one penny for the first quarter of an hour, and twopence afterwards, except when a bag has to be unsealed, when the charge is sixpence.

Letters containing money or valuables may be registered, on payment of sixpence, for which an acknowledgement is given, and the safe delivery guaranteed within the United Kingdom. Foreign letters may also be registered.

Money orders for sums not exceeding two pounds, costing threepence, and on sums above two pounds, and not exceeding five pounds, sixpence, may be had between the hours of Nine, morning, and Five, evening, (on Saturday until Six, evening), each working day. The Money Order Office is closed on Sundays.

23

Local letters posted before, or up to half-past Seven o'clock in the morning, go into the first delivery ; those posted afterwards, up to Two in the afternoon, into the second delivery.

NOTICE.—The clock at the Post-office shows railway time as observed by the Lancashire and Yorkshire Railway ; and the correct time is communicated daily from the Bolton and Manchester Station, in Trinity-street.

R. GREENHALGH, Postmaster.

LIST OF FAIRS IN LANCASHIRE.

Ashton under-Lyne, (S) Mar. 23, Ap 25, June 25, 26, 27, Nov. 21, 22, 23.—*Bartholomew*, Ap. 24, 25, Sep. 24, 25.—*Blackburn*, (W. S.) Easter M. May 11, 12, Oct.17, fortnightly fairs for cattle from the 1st Wed. bef. Feb. 2, till Mich.—*Blackrod*, first Fr. & Sat. aft. July 12—*Bolton*, (M. Th. S.) Jan. 4, July 30, 31, Oct. 13, 14, C. a fortnightly fair every second Monday—*Bootle*, (S) Ap. 26 Sep. 24.—*Broughton-in-Furness*, (W.) Ap. 27, Aug 1, Oct. 6, C.—*Burnley*, (M) March 6, Easter eve, Oct. 11, July 10, & 11, every alternate Monday.—*Bury*, (S.) Mar. 5, May, 3, Sep. 8 ; if these dates fall on Sunday, the fair is held the next day, C.—*Cartmel*, (Tu) Whit-M M. aft. Oct. 23, C. W. bef. Easter, Nov. 5 —*Chipping*, Easter Tu. Aug. 24—*Chorley*, March 26, May 5, Aug. 20, C. Oct. 21, horses, Sep. 4, 5. 6—*Chowbent*, last Th in Jan. stock, June 29, Aug. 24 ; if these dates fall on Sunday, the fair is held the next day.—*Clitheroe*, Tu March 24, 25, Aug. 2, Th and F. bef. 4th. S. aft. Sep. 22 , Dec. 7, 8, C.—*Cockerham*, March 24, C.—*Colne*, (W. S.) Mar. 7, May 13, Oct. 11, cattle last W. in every Month —*Craston*, M. bef. Shrove Tu.—*Dalton*, (S.) April 28, June 6 Oct. 23.—*Garstang*, (Th) Ap 12, Holy Th. July 10, 11.—*Great Harwood*, Mar. 3, C, Aug. 21 Hor. & C.—*Haslingden*, (Tu. S.) Feb 2, May 8, July 4, Oct 2, Easter Tu C.—*Hawkshead*, (M.) Easter M. bef. Oct. 2, C, M. bef. Ascension day, C.—*Hornby*, fortnightly fairs on Tu. June 20th, and July 30th.—*Inglewhite*, Ap. 8, Tues. bef. Holy Thurs. C—*Kirkham*, (Tu.) Feb. 4, 5, April 28, 29, Oct. 18, 19. C.—*Lancaster*, (W S.) May 1, July 5, Oct 10, C. & Ch.—*Leigh*, (S.) April 24, Dec. 7.—*Liverpool*, (W. S.) July 25, Nov. 11.—*Littleborough*, March 1, Oct. 14; 15 —*Longridge*, Feb. 16, Nov. 5, M. bef. Holy Thurs. C, April 16, March 16th, C. —*Manchester*, (Tu. Th S.) Easter week, pleasure, Oct. 1, 2, 3, C.—*Middleton*, (F.) 1st. Th. aft. March 10, 11., and April 15. 16, 2nd. Th. after Sep. 29, 30. C. &c.—*Newburgh*, June 21.—*Newton*, May 17, 18, C. Aug. 11, 12, C.—*Oldham*, (S.) May 2, July 8, 1st W. aft. Oct. 11, Th. aft, Candlemas.—*Ormskirk*, (Th.) Whit-M. Sep. 10, C.—*Padiham*, May 7, Sep. 26, C, Aug. 12, toys —*Poulton*, (M.) Feb. 3, Ap. 13, Nov. 3, C, Aug. 9, every alternate Mon. C. &c.—*Prescot*, (Tu. S.) Shrove Tu. and every second Tu. until Old May day, W. after Corpus Christi All Saints, Aug. 24, 25. Oct. 21, Nov. 1—*Preston*, (M) Jan 3 and five following days, March 27 and four following days, C. &c. Nov 7. and four following days, C, &c,—*Radcliffe Bridge*, April 29, 30, May 17, Sep. 28.—*Ribchester*, Mar. 16, Ap. 16, M. bef. Holy Th. Nov. 5, C.—*Rochdale*, (S.) May 14, Whit-Tu. Nov 7, C. fair 1st. M. in the month —*Rufford*, May 13, C.—*Standish*, June 29, Nov. 25.—*St. Helens*, (S.) M. & Tu. aft. Easter week, 1st. S. aft. Sep. 11 —*Staleybridge*, (S.) Easter Mon. Nov. 5.—*Todmorden*, (S.) Th. bef. Easter, Sep. 27. C. first Th. in every month, C.—*Turton*, July 2, 3, Sep 4, 5 —*Ulverston*, Tu. bef. Easter Sun. Oct. 7, C. &c. Nov. 12, Whit-Th. and 1st Th. aft. Oct. 23.—*Upholland*, Easter Monday —*Warrington*, (alternate W.) July 18, Nov. 30 continues ten days.— *Weeton*, M. and Tu. aft. Trinity Sunday, C.—*Wigan*, (M. F.) day before Holy Th. two following days, June 27, 28, 29, Oct. 28, horses, cattle, general wares.

INNS, HOTELS, &C.

For Beersellers see page 40 & 41.

Ainsworth Arms, C. Brownlow, Halliwell
Angel & Woolpack, Wm. Green, D'gate.
Angel, Wm. Thompson, Churchgate
Antelope, Ferdinand Ruff, Churchgate
Antelope, Thomas Taylor, Kersley
Antelope, Thos. Rogerson, Little Hulton
Archduke Charles, Thos. Windward. Blackburn street
Arrowsmith's Arms, David Morris, Well street
Bank, Thomas Knowles, Bank street
Bar Tavern, Ann Silcock, Rumworth
Bay horse, Henry Dobson, Deansgate
Bird in hand, Thomas Clough, Kersley
Bird i'th' hand, Jas. Suttle, Bank street
Black bull, John Orrel, Bradshawgate
Black horse, Jon. Grisdale, Blackhorse st
do.   John Taylor, Kersley
Blue Boar, Thomas Dickinson, D'gate
Boar's head, Jos Hardcastle, Churchgate
Boat, James Grime, Nob end
Bowling green, P. Crook, Tonge moor
do   Richard Holt, Farnworth
Bridge Inn, Wm. Tyrrell, Bridge street
Bridgewater Arms, John Shaw, Gravel Hole
Britannia, Wm. Mawde, Moor lane
Bull's Head, Wm. Sharp, Bradshawgate
do.   E. Howarth, Farnworth
Church Tavern, Lee Hall, Crook street
Clarence, Mrs. Heaton, Bradshawgate
Coach & Horses, James Edwards, D'gate
Commercial, Samuel Nuttal, Hotel street
Crofters, Thomas Thornley, Halliwell
Cross Axes, James Gorse, Deansgate
Cross Guns, R. Howarth, Blackburn str.
Cross Keys, James Raby, Cross street
do.   Francis Roskell, Churchgate
Crown Inn, Francis Baxendale, D'gate
Crown, Isaac Simpkin, Folds road
Crown & Cushion, John Thompson, Mealhouse lane
Dog, Joseph Lam, Brown street, L.B.
Dog & Patridge, John Duerden, Manor street, L.B.
Duke William, C. Greenhalgh, Cockey moor
Falcon, Robert Haslam, Kay street
Farmers' Arms, J. Holgate, Bridgman st
Farmers' Arms, T.Sugden, Darcy Lever
Flag, James Lowe, Great moor street
Fleece, Thomas Telford, Bradshawgate
Founders' Arms, Joseph Bromlow, St. George's street
Founders' Arms, Lawrence Duckworth, Ashburner street
Four Factories, John Allen, Turton str.
Four Horse Shoes, H.Wilkinson, D'gate
George, Matthias Mather, Weston street
George & Dragon, Mary Rawsthorne, Oxford street
Gibralter Rock, Alice Gerrard, Blackburn street
Golden Lion, John Haslam, Churchgate
Golden Lion, John Tonge, Farnworth
Grapes, J. Simpson, New Market place
Grey Mare, Benj. Hart, Cheapside
Hand & Banner, J. Dewhurst, Deansgate
Hare & Hounds, T. Clifford, Bank street
Hen & Chickens, Jas. Bolton, Deansgate
Horse & Groom, Elizth. Fletcher, B,gate.
Horse & Jockey, H. Dutton, Bradshawgate

Horse Shoe, Hugh Gillibrand, Manor st.
do.   Thos. Settle, New Market place
Hulton Arms, S. Worple, Over Hulton
Kenyon's Arms, Jno. Tunstall, L. Hulton
King's Arms, John Lawton, Nan lane
do.   Thomas Morris, Deansgate
King's Head, Edward Malley, Deansgate
do.   Wright Markland, Dean
Jolley Crofters, T. Pickering, St Geo's st
Lamb, James Firth, Sharples
Legs of Man, Mary Thorpe, Churchgate
Lever's Arms, Alfred Bird, Nelson square
Lord Collingwood, T. Allen, Deansgate
Lord Nelson, Rich. Mellor, Derby street
Man & Scythe, Mar. Guffog, Churchgate
Millstone, Mrs. Fisher, Crown street
Nag's Head, John Brown Holden, D'gate
Oak, Robert Allen, Churchgate
Old Hen & Chickens. W. Gregory, D'gate
Old Millstone, Joseph Kay, Deansgate
Old Nag's Head, Mar. Kirkham, D'gate
Old Three Crowns, W. S. Lomax, D'gate
Old Woolpack, J. Hardcastle, Deansgate
Pack Horse, Elizth. Hall, Bradshawgate
Pilkinton Arms, E. Smith, Derby street
Pine Apple, M. Greenhalgh, Darcy Lever
Prince Wm. John Gorton, Bradshawgate
Queen Anne, Joseph Settle, Little Lever
do.   John Silcock, Chancery lane
Queen Elizabeth, Eliz. Holt, Blkhorse st
Ram's Head, Peter Hodson, Derby street
Red Cross, Fred. Davies, Bradshawgate
Red Lion, Reuben Gorton, Deansgate
do.   James Nuttal, Crook street
do.   Elizabeth Sale, Middle Hulton
Rising Sun, W. Greenhalgh, Churchgate
Robin Hood, Sarah Beech, Lever street
Roebuck, Joseph Wallwork, Kay street
Rose and Crown, Ellis Lever, Farnwarth
do.   John Hornby, Deansgate
Rose hill, Simon Stones, Rose hill
Saddle, Betty Kirkman, Bradshawgate
St. George, John Rollinson, St Geo's st.
Seven Stars, Ann Bromley, Bank street
Shakspeare, S. Horrocks, Bradshawgate
Sir Sydney Smith, E. Howker, Bridgman street
Ship, Margaret Roscoe, Bradshawgate
Stag's Head, John Platt, Rumworth
Stork, Wm. Barcroft, Old hall street
Star, Thomas Sharples, Churchgate
Swan, J. Cork, Churchgate & B'gate.
Three Arrows, James Haslam, Old hall st
Three Crowns, Thos. Barlow, Deansgate
Three Pigeons, Thos. Beswick, Sharples
Three Tuns, Thos. Greenhalgh, Bridge st
do.   Martha Knott, Chapel street
do.   Ellen Sellers, Moor lane
Town Hall, J. Entwisle, All Saints' street
Union, Wm. Walker, Little Lever
do.   Thomas Livsey, Bullock street
Victoria, John Gillibrand, Hotel street
Vine, Peter Cort, Hotel street
Volunteer, James Knowles, Turton
do.   John Sugden, Bradshawgate
Waterloo, James Holt, Blackburn street
Wheat Sheaf, Thos. Redhead, Newport st
Wellington, Robert Lever, Garside street
White Hart, Edward Moon, Blackburn st
White Horse, S. Howarth, Mealhouse lane
York Hotel, T. Farrimond, Newport st.

Fire and Life Assurance Offices, with their Agents in Bolton·

Active: Winder and Broadbent, Bowker's row
Alliance: Cross and Greenhalgh, Acres' field
Atlas; C. Briggs, Wood street
British, Commercial, and General: R. Brownlow, Bridge street
Builders': J. W. Whittaker, Exchange street
Church of England: Rushton and Armitstead, Acres' field
County: R. Moscrop, Deansgate
Defender: William Lomax, Jun., Exchange street. (see advertisement.)
Dissenters' and General: Thomas Parkinson, Newport street, (see advertisement)
Eagle: E. Langshaw, Bowker's row
Econimic: Henry Glover, Mealhouse lane
English Widows: A. Mackie, 95, Bark street, (see advertisement
Freemasons': J. Gorton, Bowker's row
Great Britain Mutual and India and London: G. F. Wharton, Acres' Field.
Globe: J. R. Wolfenden, Silverwell street
Guardian: J. Stansfield
Legal and Commercial: T. Frankland, Bright view, Haulgh
Life Association: Henry Glover, Mealhouse lane
Liverpool: W Morris, Acres' field
Manchester: J. Knowles, Oxford st.
Medical Invalid, &c.: J. Taylor, Acres' field
North of England: J. T. Kearsley, Folds-street
Norwich Union. T. F. Heaton, Derby street
North British: T. Dawson, Chapel street, Little Bolton
Pelican Life: J. Knowles, Acres' field
Phœnix: J. Mawdsley, Market street, and J. Hulton, Bowker's row
Provident: R. Moscrop, Deansgate
Royal Exchange: Barlow and Son, Deansgate
Royal Farmers' and General: W. Hayhurst, Market street
Royal Insurance: T. Warburton, Bradshawgate
Sun: G. Cross, Market street, and A. Ferguson, Bank of Bolton
Scottish Equitable: J. Gordon, Acres' field
Scottish Union: G. J. French, Bradshawgate
Standard: J. Tickle, Bridge street
Star: Thomas Moscrop, Folds road
Temperance and General Provident Institution: J. Cunliffe, Newport street
United Kingdom: M. Dawes, Acres' field
West of England: T. Mulliner, Acres' field
Yorkshire: J. Cocksey, Gas street

Carriers from Bolton.

To ACCRINGTON. George Bromilow, from the *Cross Axes*, Monday & Thursday.

To BELMONT. Mellody, from the *Horse Shoe*, Manor street, Monday and Thursday, and by other Carriers daily; J. Halliwell, from the *Old Nag's Head*, Saturds.

To BLACKBURN. Robert Atkin, from the *Bird-i'th'-hand*, Monday, Wednesday, and Friday; and by Railway.

To BURY AND ROCHDALE. Robert Greenhalgh, from the *Boar's Head*, Tuesday Thursday, and Saturday; Eleanor Scholfield, to Bury and Heywood, from the same house, Monday and Thursday; John Ratcliffe, from the *Man and Scythe*, daily and by Railway.

To CHORLEY. C. and H. Sherrington, from the *Bay Horse*, Monday, Wednesday and Friday; and by Railway.

To DARWEN. Robert Atkin, from the *Bird-i'th'-hand*, Monday, Wednesday, and Friday; Ralph Entwisle, from the *Fleece*, Thursdays and Saturdays; and by Railway

To EDENFIELD. Rd. Brierley, from the *Old Nag's Head*, Monday and Thursday.

To HINDLEY. James Meadows, from the *Three Crowns*, daily.

To HASLINGDEN. Robert Whittaker, from the *Cross Axes*, Monday and Thursday

To HEYWOOD. Elleanor Scholfield, from the *Boar's head*, Monday and Tnursday

To HORWICH AND RIVINGTON. Lee and Kershaw, from the *King's Arms*, every Thursday.

To LITTLE LEVER. Abraham Longworth and Peter Heywood, from the *Man & Scythe*, daily; Samuel Warburton, and Dan Yates, from the BOAR'S HEAD, every Monday, Wednesday, and Friday.

To PRESTON. C. and H. Sherrington, from the BAY HORSE, Monday, Wednesday, and Friday; also by Railway.

To RADCLIFFE. Samuel Warburton, and Dan Yates, from the BOAR'S HEAD, Monday, Wednesday, and Friday; and James Mather, from the *Man and Scythe*, Monday and Saturday.

To SUMMERSEAT. Richard Tattersall, from the BIRD-I'TH'-HAND, every Monday

To TYLDESLEY. Richard Harrison, from the BAY HORSE, Monday, Thursday, and Saturday; John Partington, from HIGHER NAG'S HEAD, every Monday; and James Meadows, from the THREE CROWNS, daily; John Atkin, from the CROSS AXES, Monday and Thursday.

To WIGAN. Peter Southworth, from the Higher Nag's Head, daily; and Railway.

An Historical Sketch of Bolton.

◄—◆—►

BOLTON, is a Market Town and Corporate and Parliamentary Borough, 6 miles W.S.W. of Bury, 11 miles N.W. of Manchester, 12 miles S. of Blackburn, 11 miles S.E. of Chorley, and 197 miles from London. It consists of two townships, Great and Little Bolton, divided by a small rivulet which runs at the bottom of a deep valley from E. to W. The distinctive name is derived from its ancient situation on the Moors. Bolton has grown into great importance within the last seventy years, and in its degree keeps pace with Manchester. A variety of causes have combined to produce this effect, but the principal are its vicinity to the metropolis of the cotton trade, the abundant supply of excellent coal with which it is surrounded, and its direct railway communication.

The Manor of Bolton is of considerable antiquity. Roger de Maresey sold this manor with his other lands between the rivers Ribble and Mersey, to Ranulf de Blunderville, Earl of Chester, for 240 marks of Silver, and a pair of white gloves to be presented annually at Easter; and William, Earl of Ferrers, of Groby, died *seized* of the Lordship, of which this was a part in the 16th of Edward I. In the 4th of Edward III. the possessions were still inherited by the house of Ferrers, but they afterwards passed into the family of the Pilkingtons.

Leonard Pilkington, Lord of Pilkington, in Lancashire, lived in 10 Henry I. From Leonard descended Alexander, who was living 46 Henry III. and 7 Edward I. and had issue Sir Roger, Lord of Pilkington, to whom he gave Rivington. The last-named Sir Roger and Sir Adam Hoghton were Knights of the Shire in the 39 Edward III. From Sir Roger descended Sir Thomas Pilkington, Lord of Bury and Pilkington, who was high Sheriff for the County of Lancaster in the 3d, 5th, 13th, and 26th of Edward IV. but who for adhering to the cause of Richard III. at the battle of Bosworth-field, was in the 1st of Henry VII. attainted and beheaded, and his estates were confiscated and given to Thomas Lord Stanley, then created Earl of Derby.

In the reign of Henry VIII. Leland gives the following description of Bolton:---" Bolton upon Moore Market" says he, " standeth most by cottons, and course yarne. Divers villages in the moores about *Bolton* do make *cottons*. Nother the site nor the ground abowte *Bolton* is so good as it is abowte *Byri*. They burne at *Bolton* sum canale, but more se cole, of the wich, the pittes be not far of. They burne turfe also." Blome who wrote about a century after, says---" Boulton, seated on the river Irwell, a fair well built town, with broad streets, hath a market on Mondays, which is very good for *clothing* and *provisions;* and it is a place of great trade for *fustians*."

AN HISTORICAL SKETCH OF BOLTON.

During the civil wars of Charles 1. this town witnessed more of the horrors of war than any other place in the county of Lancaster. The main body of the inhabitants, like those of Manchester, embraced the cause of the parliament, and till the spring of the year 1644, a garrison in that interest was maintained in this place. On the appearance of Prince Rupert in the north, the works at Bolton, which consisted principally of a thick mud wall, defended by cannon, and surrounded with a wide and deep fosse, were materially strengthened, and Colonel Rigby who had been for three months engaged in the seige of Lathom House, retreated with his army of two thousand men to this place. The prince, whose first object was to raise the seige of Lathom, having effected that purpose by his approach at the head of 10,000 men, marched to Bolton, where he arrived on the 28th of May, 1664, and was joined by the Earl of Derby from the Isle of Man. By two o'clock in the afternoon of that day, the whole force was assembled on the moor at the south-west of the town. Here a council of war was called, and it was resolved to carry the place by storm. The assault was made with great gallantry and resolution, but being met with equal firmness on the part of the garrison, consisting now of 3,000 troops, the assailants were obliged to retreat, under a galling fire of cannon and musketry, and with a loss of 200 men. A second council of war was now called and a second onset resolved upon. The Earl of Derby, feeling how much the future safety of his own family, and the interests of the loyal cause were concerned in the issue, requested the prince to allow him two companies of his old soldiers, under the command of Colonel Tyldesley, and to confide to his lordship the post of honour, which was to command the van, declaring that he would either carry the town or leave his body in the ditch. With this request the prince complied reluctantly, from a disinclination to hazard a person of so much consequence in so dangerous a service. After due preparation the prince gave orders for the second assault, and the Earl of Derby at the head of his 200 Lancashire men, principally his tenants and their sons, marched directly to the walls; here the conflict was again renewed with desperate resolution on both sides; but the earl overcame all opposition, and entering the town at the *private Akers* carried consternation and dismay into the whole garrison." The cry was now set up of " Save himself who can" *Sauve qui peut*---as the French have it. The Royal forces rushed into every quarter of the town, put great numbers to the sword, pursuing their victory not only in the town but some miles round, killing, destroying and spoiling almost all they met, and as the inhabitants allege, denying quarter and using other violences, besides totally plundering the town, and slaying four ministers.

After the disasterous battle of Worcester, fought between Cromwell and Prince Charles, afterwards Charles II. the Earl of Derby was made prisoner in Cheshire by Major Edge, on his way into Lancashire, and being brought to trial before a military tribunal at Chester, upon a charge of treason against the commonwealth, he was sentenced to die at Bolton.

He was executed on Wednesday, the 15th of October, 1651. On the scaffold he preserved the equanimity of his deportment; and having justified himself from the charge of being a man of blood, and professed his unshaken allegiance to his king, he laid his neck upon the block exclaiming with great energy—" The Lord bless my wife and children, and the Lord bless us all." He then gave the signal, and the executioner struck of his head at a blow, while many of the spectators testified their grief by sobs and prayers.

The age of invention now commenced, and the town of Bolton took its full share in the race of enterprize and improvement. The most distinguished of all the early manufacturers, by the aid of machinery, was a resident, though not a native of this place, and Richard Arkwright, a humble barber, was destined by the revolution of fortune, and the revolution of his own spindles, to rank amongst the worthies of Bolton. In 1780, the spinning jenny, and the water frame, found their way into pretty general use; and Samuel Crompton, an inhabitant of the parish of Bolton, residing in part of an old mansion called " The Hall i'th' Wood," produced a machine which combined the principles of the two machines, and was called from that circumstance, a *Mule*. This valuable invention he gave to the public in the year 1780, and a small subscription amounting to about one hundred guineas served rather to express the sense of obligation felt by the manufacturers than to reward the ingenious mechanic. About twenty years afterwards, when the utility of the machine was more fully ascertained, another subscription was opened for him, and the sum of £400 was added to the former acknowledgement. In 1812 the merit of Samuel Crompton's machine was brought by petition under the consideration of parliament, and the sum of £5000 was awarded to the inventor out of the public purse. In 1824 the Steam power used in Bolton was equal to 1446 horses; at present it is estimated at upwards of 3000 horses' power.

The Reform Bill conferred upon Bolton the elective franchise, with the right of sending two Members to Parliament. The present representatives are Dr. John Bowring, of Westminster, and Stephen Blair, Esq., a townsman.

The Municipal Act of 1838, incorporated Bolton, and it now has Mayor, Aldermen, Council, and Borough Magistrates. The following list shows the gentlemen, who have filled the high office of Chief Magistrate :--

1838-9.. C. J. Darbishire, Esq.	1844-5.. John Slater, Esq.
1839-40.. Robt. Heywood, Esq.	1845-6.. Stephen Blair, Esq.
1840-1. Jas. Arrowsmith, Esq.	1846-7.. James Scowcroft, Esq
1841-2.. Thomas Cullen, Esq.	1847-8.. Ridgway Bridson, Esq
1842-3.. Robert Walsh, Esq.	1848-9.. T. L. Rushton, Esq.
1843-4.. Thomas Gregson, Esq.	

The Churches and Chapels are numerous and respectable, and so also are the public institutions, of all which we give a list in another part.

We give the following verbatim from Baine's " History of Bolton," to which we are indebted for most of our information, as a true picture of Bolton in 1825.

"The spirit of public improvement was perhaps never so high in Bolton as at the present moment: three new squares are laid out in different parts of the town; namely, the New-square between Oxford-street and Newport.street, which is now nearly completed, and the area of which is to be used as a market-place; Nelson-square, formed in 1823, at one end of which the Dispensary is situated; and Bradford-square, at the bottom of Bradshawgate, is planned and ready for buildings. No fewer than four hundred and twenty-eight new houses were erected in Great Bolton in the year 1823, and one hundred and ninety-six were erected in Little Bolton in the same year. A handsome public building to be called the Exchange Buildings, is about to be erected by public subscription in the Market-place; and a new Town Hall is projected in the same square for the transaction of magisterial and other public business. A new Assembly Room, of ample dimensions, has recently been built in Oxford-street; and the town also numbers a Theatre and Concert Rooms amongst its public buildings. A handsome Town Hall has just been finished in St. George's-street, in Little Bolton, at a cost of £2000, defrayed by the trustees of that township. A Gas Light Company was established here on the 4th of March 1819, and the town was first lighted with that brilliant vapour on the 1st of May 1819. The works give name to a street in Moor-lane, and they are constructed on a judicious scale of 40,000 feet of gas. The extent of the population and trade of this town and neighbourhood had for some years demanded a public communication, and on the 5th of July, 1823, a Newspaper was published in Bolton, by Mr. J. Yates, for the first time, under the title of " The Bolton Express," which continues to be issued every Saturday morning. One very essential improvement remains yet to be effected : the inhabitants have long been insufficiently supplied with water; but on the 17th of June, 1824, the Royal assent was given to an act "for supplying with water the towns of Great and Little Bolton, and the township of Sharples, in the Parish of Bolton-le-Moors."

" The progress of population has been very rapid in Bolton: in the year 1773, soon after the time when cotton machinery began to be introduced, the number of inhabitants in Great and Little Bolton, amounted to 5,339; in 1789, they had increased to 11,740; in 1801, to 17,416; in 1811, to 24,149; in 1821, 31,295; and it is probable that at present, 1825, they are little short of 40,000." Present population, 1848, 70,000.

The parish of Bolton whether considered with relation to its early history or to its improving condition, is a highly interesting portion of the kingdom, and this town ranks deservedly as the second manufacturing place in the county of Lancaster, and the sixteenth town in point of population in England.

MISCELLANEOUS STATISTICS OF THE BOROUGH OF BOLTON,

For the Year ending August 31st., 1848.

The area of the Borough of Bolton is about 2¾ square miles, and contained at the census, in June, 1841, 52,380 inhabitants. The gross annual value of rateable property is £162,215 14s. 8d. The Police Force numbers 24 men; the cost of which, last year was £1,168 0s. 2d.; making a cost per head upon the whole population of about 5¼d.

Dwelling Houses, inhabited 8010	Houses supposed to sell liquors without Licence , ... 15
Do. uninhabited.... 319	
Cellars in Great Bolton, occupied.. 1208	Public-houses and beer-houses where thieves and prostitutes resort.... 20
Do. do, unoccupied 112	Do. where gambling is practised 13
Do. occupied as warehouses.. 233	Do. having musical entertainments 14
Do. in Little Bolton, occupied 485	
Do. do. unoccupied 20	Do. dancing beside music...... 11
Do. occupied as warehouses.. 50	Houses where prostitutes reside 41
New Buildings erected during the last two years:	Houses for the resort of thieves.... 35
Dwelling Houses, 357; Shops, 5; Warehouses, 2; Chapels, 2; Schools, 4; Workshops, 1; Baths, 1; total, ... 426	Houses for the reception of stolen property 81
	Mendicant lodging houses 81
	Do. where the sexes sleep indiscriminately in one room .. 74
Factories, 54; Steam Power, 2,200; hands employed, 8,262	Reputed thieves—males 79; females 35
Foundries, 21; Steam Power, 590; hands employed, 2,447.	Prostitutes in the Borough 138
Bleach Crofts, 8; Steam Power 628; hands employed, 1035.	Pawnbrokers 20
	Public Fire Engines 5
Paper Mill and Gas Works; Steam, Power, 124; hands employed, 133.	Firemen 22
Coal Mines, 5; Steam Power, 85; hands employed, 179.	Fires 23
	Probable amount of Property destroyed .... £5,330 15s. 0d.
Public Houses 117	In only 14 of the cases were the parties insured
Beer houses, selling on the premises 188	Inquests held by the Borough Coroner 71
Do. selling off the premises 11	

A LIST
OF THE PRINCIPAL STREETS AND LANES IN BOLTON.

EXCHANGE WARD.

Acres field	Coronation street	Joiners' square	Oxford street
Ashburner street	Crown street	King street	Queen street
Bamber's court	Cunliffe's court	Knowsley street	Ridgway gates
Bank street	Deansgate	Lottery row	Shambles
Barn street	Dog row	Makinson's square	Ship gates
Blackhorse street	Exchange st. east	Market street	Simpson square
Bold street	Exchange st. west	Mawdsley street	Spring gardens
Bowker's row	Folds street	Mechanic street	Taylor brow
Bradshawgate	Foundry square	Nelson square	Velvet walks
Bridge street	Frank's yard	New Market place	Water street
Chancery lane	Great Moor street	Newport street	White Lion brow
Chapel alley	Grime street	New row	Woods' court
Cheapside	Hotel street	Old acres	
Cooper street	Howell croft	Old hall street	

BRADFORD WARD.

Bleackley street	Foundry street	Milk street	Slater field
Bridgman street	Gregson field	Nelson street	Stott hillock
Bull lane	High field house	Newport terrace	Sunning hill
Burnden	High street	Orlando street	Swan lane
Carey street	Hill street	Pilkington street	Sweet green
Claremont	Horrocks court	Pitt street	The Height
Coe street	Houghton street	Rose hill	The Pike
Crook street	Lever street	Rothwell street	Treacle row
Derby street	Manchester road	Shakspeare's court	Wellington place
Fitton's houses	Martin's buildings	Shaw street	Weston street
Fletcher street	Martin's houses	Sidney street	York street

DERBY WARD.

Baldwin street
Balshaw street
Blackburn street
Blackhorse street
Bridge house
Bright terrace
Bristol street
Bull field
Cannon street
Chamberhall
Cobden place
Commission street
Coronation square
Crook street
Dale street
Deansgate
Defence street
Derby street
Duncan street
Ebenezer street
Flash street
Frederic street
Gas street
Garside street
Gilnow
Great bridge
Greenstreet
Grime's lot
Hanover street
Hanover square
James street
John street
Kay street
Little bridge house
Lodge vale
Lupton street
Maire street
Markland street
Middle street
Moor lane
Noble street
Pike's buildings
Pike's lane
Pump houses
Punch street
Salt pie row
School street
Shuttle street
Spaw lane
Stable row
Stanley street
Taylor court
Taylor fold
Three arrow's sqr.
Walker fold
Ward street
Weston street
Willows

CHURCH WARD.

Andrew street
Bank street
Baron entry
Blackhorse street
Bowling green]
Bradford place
Bradford terrace
Bradshawgate
Bradshaw street
Bridgman place
Bridgman street
Byng street
Chapel street
Charlesacre brow
Church bank
Churchgate
Church wharf
Collier's row
Crook street
Cross street
Dawes' street
Glaizbrook lane
Great Moor street
Gush place
Haulgh cottage
Haulgh bridge
Haulgh hall
High bank
Johnson street
Lane ends
Lever grove
Lever street
Lomax buildings
Newport place
Newport square
Newport street
Old acres
Oliver lane
Openshaw croft
Orlando street
Ormrod street
Princess street
Raike's works
Railway streeet
Retreat place
Rose hill
Rose place
Silverwell house
Silverwell street
Spring field
Squint lane
Strawberry hill
Sweet green
Trinity street
Union buildings
Vale bank
Victoria terrace
West brook
West brook house
Weston street
Wood street
Wheatfield

EAST WARD.

Ainsworth court
Bank court
Bank house
Barlow street
Barlow row
Barn square
Barn street
Baron street
Bold street
Bolton's court
Bradshaw street
Brown street
Bullock street
Burton court
Burton street
Bury street
Cable street
Chapel street
Charles street
Church wharf
Cooper's row
Crompton street
Cross street
Dean street
Fairfield—High st.
Folds
Foldscottage
Foundry square
Foundry street
Garden street
George's court
Geo. terrace, folds
Goodfellow's ter-
race, folds
Goodwin street
Green bank
Green street
High street
Hulme street
Independent street
Kay street
Kestor fold
Kestors
Lee street
Leigh street
Lever street
Little Bolton hall
Lomax buildings
Lum street
Manor street
Mechanic street
Middle street
Mill hill
Mill hill place
Milk street
Mill street
Monks row
Morris street
Naylor row
Oliver row
School street
Slater street
Smith street
Smithy street
Tipping place
Tipping street
Union street
Water street
Well street
William street
Waterloo street
Wellington court

WEST WARD.

All Saints street
Back lane
Back o'th' Bank
Bark street east
Bark street west
Bath street
Blackburn street
Bow street
Bridge street
Brinks place
Chemist street
China lane
China street
Chorley new road
Chorley street
Church street
Clarence street
Cooper's street
Cooper's square
Croasdale street
Crofts
Crown street
Dale street
Dawson lane
Dawson street
Dukes street
Duncan street
Falcon street
Flax place
Gleam street
Green heys
Grundyfold, Kay st.
Hadwin street
Haigh street
Halliwell road
Hart street

Harwood street	Morris square	St. Georges street	Waterloo
Hyde street	Mort field	St. Georges terrace	Waterloo fold
Gilnow	Nelson street	St. Helena	Waterloo street
Gleave street	Oswald street	School hill	Waterside
Kensington place	Parkhill	Simpson street	Wellington cottage
Lodge street	Parkhill place	Slater street	West cottage
Lynes court	Prince street	Taylor street	West street
Mere hill	Rothwell street	Vernon house	Wood street
Morris row	St. Georges place	Vernon bank	

PLACES OF WORSHIP WITH THEIR DATES OF BUILDING.

The figures on the left refer to the Ministers who preach in them: see Clergy list; those on the right to the time of building.

---

1 *Albert Place Chapel*; Independent; 1846.
2 *All Saints' Church*, All Saints' street, L. B.; Episcopalian; 1740,
3 *Bank street Chapel*; Unitarian; 1689.
4 *Baptist Chapel*, Moor lane; 1822.
  Baptist Chapel, King street; (various ministers) 1832.
5 *Bridge street Chapel*; Wesleyan; 1803.
6 *Christ Church*, Blackburn street; Episcopalian; 1819.
  Duke's Alley Chapel; Independent; without regular minister at present; 1754
7 *Emanuel Church*, Cannon street; Episcopalian.
8 *Fletcher street Chapel*; Wesleyan; 1819.
  Friend's Meeting House, Tipping place; (various ministers) 1820.
  Independent Methodist Chapel, Folds road; (various ministers) 1823.
9 *Mawdsley street Chapel*; Independent; 1807.
  Methodist New Connexion, Lever street; 1836.
  New Jerusalem Chapel, Higher Bridge street; without regular min. at present
10 *Primitive Methodist Chapel*, Newport street. 1822
11 *Primitive Methodist Chapel*, Higher Bridge street, L. B.
  Refugees Chapel, Hanover street; Wesleyan; (various ministers) 1834
12 *Ridgway Gates Chapel*; Wesleyan; 1776.
13 *St. Andrew's Church*, Bowkers row; Presbyterian; 1846.
14 *St. George's Church*, L. B.; Episcopalian; 1796.
15 *St. John's Church*, (erecting near Mill hill, L. B.); Episcopalian.
16 *St. Marie's Chapel*, St. George's road; Roman Catholic; 1847
17 *St. Peter's (or Parish) Church*, Churchgate; Episcopalian.
18 *St. Peter and St. Paul's*, Pilkington street; Roman Catholic; 1800.
19 *Trinity Church*, Trinity street; Episcopalian; 1823
20 *Tong Moor District Chapel*, Tong moor (erecting)
21 *Wesleyan Association Chapel*, Bowker's row; 1846.

Established Churches - - - - - - - - - 8
All classes of Dissenters- - - - - - - - - 20

Total Places of Worship in Bolton- - - -28

The Population of Great and Little Bolton in 1841 was nearly 50,000, which divided by 28, the number of places of worship of every denomination, gives 1785 of a congregation to each. As the population has much increased since 1841, the disproportion of Church and Chapel accommodation to what are, or should be, the wants of the Borough, is still greater.

Halls, Public Offices, &c.,

Assembly Rooms, Swan Hotel, Bradshawgate
Barracks, Garside-street; barrack-master,
  62d Regt.—Officers, Colonel Shortt, Rose hill; Capt. Young, do. Lieu. Cox, Ensigns Wood, and Seale, Blackburn road
Bolton Advertiser Office, Mealhouse-lane
Bolton Chronicle Office, Bradshawgate
Bolton & Kenyon (North Western Line) Railway Co. Passenger station, Great Moor-street; Goods station, Blackhorse-street—Manager, Mr. Bradshaw, St. George's place; Superintendent, Mr. James Nicholson, Crook-st. Clerk at Goods station, Mr. Barnes, Blackhorse-street; Clerk at the Passenger station, Mr. John Diggle, Bridgeman place

Bolton and Manchester Passenger and Goods station, Trinity-st.; Goods Superintendent, Mr. Joseph Taylor, Burnden; Inspector, Mr. James Douling, Derby-st.; Clerks, Mr Thos. Hodson, Higher Bridge-st.; Mr David Barber, Sidney-st.; Mr James Crowshaw, Rose hill; Mr John Bamber, Haulgh Hall; Mr John Lomax, Barnes-street

Bolton and Preston Passenger and Goods station, same as above

Bolton and Blackburn Passenger and Goods station.—Goods Superintendent, Mr Joseph Ramsbottom, Cockerill spring; the others same as above.

Bolton, Bury, Wigan, and Liverpool Passenger and Goods station, same as the Bolton and Manchester

Bolton Waterworks Co. (Old proprietors,) Silverwell-street : Mr Wolfenden, Secretary.

Bolton Waterworks Co. (Mayor, Burgesses, &c,) Acres' Field : Manager, Mr Thomas Green, Rose hill; Clerk, Mr Abraham Isherwood, Back lane; Collector, Mr Luke Boardman, Back lane.

Borough Coroner's Office, Acres' Field, Mr John Taylor, Ainsworth Hall, Coroner

Borough Treasurers Office, Mr Wolfenden's Silverwell-street

Borough Prosecutor's Office, Mawdsley-street; Mr John Gaskill, Prosecutor

Billeting Office, Bowker's row; Mr J. Harris, Ridgway gates, Billet Master

Baths, Bridgeman st. John Darbyshire, Esq. Banker, Treas.; Richard Badger, Esq. Rose hill, Sub-Treas.; Thomas Andrews, Esq. Acres' Field, Secy. John Brown, Esq. Churchgate, Assistant Secy.; James Pollitt, Manager.

Concert and Assembly Rooms, over the Baths

County Sessions Room, Town Hall, *l. b.*

Cloth Hall, Market-st.

County Court's Office, Acres' field, Mr Holden, Summerfield, Clerk

Clerk of the Peaces' Office, Acres' field, Mr John Gordon, Chorley newroad

Clerks to the Magistrates, Messrs. Langshaw, Winder, and Briggs, at their respective offices.

Dispensary, Nelson square, Mr Jackson, house Surgeon.—Patients admitted since 1815, 76,372

Exchange Reading Room, Market place.—Annual payment, 25s.

Excise Office, Bowker's row, Excise officers,—Supervisor, John Bryant, Esq. 6, Blackburn st. G. B. Officers, Mr George Brooks, 19, Falcon-st. L.B. Mr Benjamin Morgan, Derby-st. G. B.; Mr George Beech, Orlando-st. Manchester road; Mr Benjamin Milnes, 9, Bath-st. L. B.; Mr Hugh Holden, Bridgman-st. G. B. HALSHAW MOOR, Mr James Saunders; ASTLEY BRIDGE, Mr Robert K. Jollie.

Fire Engine Station, Town's yard, Falcon-st. Mr R. Nicholson, bk. Bridge-st

Fire Engine Station, Old Hall-st. Superint., Mr H. Higson, 20, Bridge-st The Runner resides in old Hall-st. to whom notice of Fires should be given, or at the Police Station, Bowker's row

Gas Light and Coke Co's Office, Gas-st. Moor lane : Mr Thomas Green, Manager, Albert-place; Mr George Nurse, Cashier, New Market place; Mr John Hampson, Lee, Collector, *Clarence-st. L. B.*

Guardians' Office, Acres' field. *(For particulars, see Page 18.)*

Inspector of Weights and Measures Office, (for Borough,) Chancery lane, James Fogg, Water-street.

Inspector of Weights and Measures, Office, (for County,) Bradshawgate, Mr Butcher, Bradshawgate.

Mechanics' Institution, Bridge-st.; P. Ainsworth, Esq. Smithills Hall, President; Mr J. Entwisle, Defence-street, Secretary; Mr Joseph Kirkham, Librarian.—The following is a list of Periodicals, &c., that are taken in :—

Quarterly Review	Metropolitan Magazine	Chemical Gazette
Westminster do.	Fraser's do.	Family Economist
Edinburgh do.	New Monthly do.	
Chambers' Journal	Bentley's Miscellany	
Peoples' do.	Hogg's Weekly Instructor	NEWSPAPERS :—
Practical Mechanics' do.	Land we live in	Illustrated London News
Mechanics' Magazine	Athenæum	Globe
Hood's do.	Mirror	Daily News
Ainsworth's do.	Punch	Bolton Chronicle
Philosophical do.	History of Pendennis	Liverpool Mercury
Blackwood's do.	Man made of Money	Manchester Guardian
Tait's do.	The Lancet	Ditto Examiner & Times
Dublin University do.		

TERMS :—*Hon: Members having two cards (one transferable) £1 1s. per annum—General Members 2s. 6d. per quarter.*

Offices for taking Acknowledgments of Married Women, (see Attornies.)
Overseers' Office for Great Bolton, Folds st.; (see almanack, page 18.)
Overseers' and Trustees' Office for Little Bolton, Town Hall; (see do.)
Post Office, Bradshawgate; (see almanack, page 23, 24, & 33.)
Police Office, Bowker's row; *Superintendent,* James Harris; Thos. Beech,
   Lever street; Martin Finnigan, Foundry square; James Grime, back Union street;
   Thomas Newburn, Coe street, Sergeants.
Police Office, (County) Town Hall; Andrew Milne, *Supt.;* T. King, *Sergt.*
Reform News Room, Folds street; John Maloney, Room-keeper.
Savings' Bank, Market street; (see banks, page 2.)
Stamp Office, Deansgate; Mr John Heaton, Bradford terrace, Agent.
Sunday School Reading-room, Acres'-field; Mr Wm. Milligan Cheapside,
   Treas.; Mr A. Mackie, *Secy.*—London Times, Daily News and Express.
   Glasgow Examiner, Record, Patriot, Manchester Examiner and Times, Guardian,
   and Liverpool Mercury, *twice a week*—The Illustrated News, Nonconformist,
   Wesleyan, Watchman, British Banner, Standard of Freedom, Jerrold's Newspaper,
   Manchester Courier, Leeds Mercury, and Bolton Chronicle, (two copies) *weekly.*
The Magazines are numerous, and represent all the bodies of Evangelical Christians.
TERMS:—Senior Scholars, 9d; Teachers, Ministers, and Lay Preachers, 1s; Others,
   1s. 6d; per quarter.
Tax Office, Wood street; (see page 22)
Temperance Hall, L.B., (length, 26 yds.; breadth, 21 yds.) It accommo-
   dates to tea 800 persons; standing room for 3,500; sitting room for 1,500.—
   Cost of building, £2,200; erected 1839. Hall-keeper, Thomas Roscoe, 34, Lever
   street, L.B. Application for the hall should be made to Mr John Cunliffe, Wire-
   worker, Newport st; Mr John Wright, Deansgate; and to Mr Baron, Bradshawgate
Theatre, Mawdsley street.
Town Hall, St George's street; holds 400. Application to be made to Mr
   Phineas Hall, Falcon street, or Mr T. Entwisle, Green hill
Town Clerk's Office, Acres' field; James Knowles, Esq., Clerk.
   Mr Lansley, Bark street, Assistant
Workhouse, Fletcher st., Job Harrison, *Master;* Betty Harrison, *Matron.*

𝕭olton 𝕻ost 𝕺ffice.—*See also Almanack, page* 23 & 24.

Robert Greenhalgh, Wood-street, Postmaster.

Gilbert Whalley, Deansgate, Clerk.

William Jones, Great Moor-street, Clerk.

Letter Carriers.

Thomas Murray, Union buildings	George Bleakley, York-street
John Smith, Squint lane	John France, Taylor fold, Moor lane

Country Post Messengers.

Henry Orrell, Union buildings	James Crompton, back Andrew-st.
John Duckworth, Bank-street	Isaiah Fletcher, Bold-street, G. B.
John Hill, Bold-street, L. B.	William Pilling, Crook-street

Great Bolton Receiving House.

Thomas Chambers, Moor-lane.

Little Bolton Receiving House.

William Thirlwind, Kay-street.

Country Receiving Houses.

		Receivers.		Messengers.	
Horwich	..		Thomas Fell	..		Henry Orrell
Turton	..		John Butterworth	..		John Duckworth
Egerton	..		James Mayoh	..		Do.
Ringley	..		William Dean	..		John Hill
Breightmet	..		John Brooks	..		James Crompton
Farnworth	..		John Nuttall	..		Isaiah Fletcher
Little Hulton	..		John Urmston	..		Do.
Westhoughton	..		Mary Grundy	..		William Pilling

A LIST OF SUNDAY SCHOOLS.

*Those marked thus * have given official reports; the others are as near us can be ascertained.*

NAMES OF SCHOOLS.	NAMES OF SUPERINTENDENTS.	NAMES OF SECRETARIES.	Male Tch.	Fem. Tch.	Total of Teachers.	Boys.	Girls.	} TOTAL.	TOTAL IN 1825.	No. of Bks. in Library
* Albert Place Chapel	Rev. David Nimmo, Bath street	Mr. F. B. Milnes, Bath street	14	10	24	120	90	210		100
* All Saint's Chapel	Mr. William Holt, 8, Green street	Mr. W. Holt, 8, Green street	14	14	28	180	165	345	200	233
* Association Chapel	Mr. Joseph Broughton, King street	Mr. Baron, Bradshawgate	20	12	32	200	241	441		495
* Bank street Chapel	Rev. F. Baker, Fairfield house	Mr. Richard Fairclough, Bulfield, and Mr. David Byers, do	8	10	18	77	110	187	130	300
* Baptist (Moorlane)	Mr. George Henry, Park hill, and Mr. John Mather, Binks brow		17	18	35	133	195	328	200	
* Christ Church	Mr. James Mercer, Weston street, and Mr. William Hughes, Bradshawgate		16	12	28	190	210	400	480	500
* Dukes Alley	Mr. Adam Ferguson, Bolton Bank	Mr. James Nicholson, Crook st., & Mr. Joseph Brierley Orlando st.	25	19	44	253	286	539	450	
Emanuel Church	No return		10	10	20	90	110	200		
* Fletcher street	Mr. R. Ormrod, 1, Cannon street, and Mr. J. Bommer, 22, Commission street	Mr. Peter Ormrod, 1, Cannon st.	24	23	47	344	406	750	114	466
Wesleyan Branch { * Moss st. Pike's lane	Mr. John Thornley, 10, Derby street, and Mr. S. Markland, Pike's lane	Mr. W. Thornley, 10, Derby street	17	10	27	86	103	189		230
* Slater field	Mr. Adam Edge, 6, James street	Mr. R. Horrocks, 11, Knowsley st.	13	5	18	88	111	199		228
* Willows	Mr. John Hart, 117, Derby street, and Mr. James Horridge, Walker fold	Mr. J. Dainty, 7, Back Fletcher st.	7	1	8	50	57	107		72
* Free Gospel Sunday School	Mr. John Ridings, back Baron street	Messrs. Ridings and Booth, back Baron street	8	3	11	30	40	70		34
Friends	No return		5	5	10	40	60	100		
* Independent Methodist	Mr. George Winterburn, Ridgway Gates, and Mr. Thomas Bramwell, Smith street	Mr. John Winterburn, Ridgway Gates	34	26	60	270	356	626	350	537
S* Lever street Chapel	Mr. C. Needham, Howel croft	Mr. J. Bradley, Great Moor st.	8	5	13	78	85	163		148
* Mawdsley street Chapel	Mr. John Hamilton, Newport place, and Mr. Wm. Brown, Bourne street	Mr. W. Scholes, Hotel street	19	20	39	221	262	483	500	650
* Rose hill (Branch of last)	Mr. James Haddock, Bradshawgate	Mr. John Wharton, Bradshawgate	12	5	17	57	78	135		108
* New Jerusalem Chapel	Mr. John Pickering, 23. Spaw lane	Mr. Isaac Low, Foundry street	12	3	15	30	44	74	150	59

School / Chapel	Teachers / Managers								
								96	
								90	200
								800	1700
*Primitive Methodist Chapel, Higher bridge street	Mr. W. Bury, back of "Waterloo," and Mr. John Drenan, Kestor fold	11	9	20	73	84	157	130	940
*Primitive Methodist Chapel, Newport street	Mr. Stpn. Downs, Spring gardens	14	3	17	60	70	500	101	920
*Bidgway Gates	Mr. W. Bidy	47	53	100	440	500	500	920	1320
*Refugees' Chapel	Mr. John Robertshaw, Crook street, No. 9	8	6	52	48	53	670	150	370
*Saint Andrew's Church	Mr. James Wardle, Bark street, and Mr. Thomas Taylor, Park hill place; Mr J. Cannon, Park hill; Mr J.Scholfield, Kay st: Mr T.Knowles, Weston st: and Mr Samuel Hunt, Commission st:	30	40	14	420	500	80	210	1000
*Saint George's Church	Mr. James Bell, Bark street; Mr. Pendlebury, Market street; Mr. Foster, Bath street, and Mr. John Green, Rose hill	60	39	70	650	670	1320	1350	300
*St. Peter's, Parish Church	Mr. Phineas Hall, Falcon street, and Mr. Joseph Spencer, Orlando street; & Mr. J. Spencer, Orlando street	6	6	99	70	80	150		150
*Saint John's	Rev. W. Chamberlain, Folds road	22	19	12	160	210	370		160
*Trinity Church	Mr. Thomas Joules, Andrew street, and Mr. O. Greenhalgh, Andrew street; Mr. S. Worthington, Lever street			441					
TOTALS....		481	386	917	4403	5176	10079	6824	6556

ACADEMIES & PUBLIC SCHOOLS.

*Those marked thus * are Boarding Schools.*

Aspinwall, Margaret, Wood street
Antrobus, James, Vernon Bank, r Bath street
Barnes, James, Edgworth
Beswick, Mary, 56, Higher Bridge street
*Bostock Eliza, St. George's place
British School, Higher Bridge street.—Master: J. F. Mc' Farlane, r Moor lane. Mistress: Anne Mayell, r All Saint's street
Bulmer, Jane, Lever street
Catholic School, Pilkington street.—Master: M. Kelly, Mist: M. Byrne, & M. Wignall.
* Cooper, Mary and Jane, Kearsley Cottage
*Crossland, Sarah, Orlando street
Cunliffe, James, Hulme street, L. B.
Fell, Elizabeth, Mount Pleasant. Well st., L.B.
Fisher, Henry, Hanover street, r Moor lane
Fortune, Joshua, Edgworth
Gordon, John, Silverwell street, r Rose hill
Grammar School, Church bank.—Mas: Rev.D. S. Hodgson, Pembroke place, and J. C. Airey, St. George's terrace
* Harper, Ellen, 143 & 144, Higher Bridge st.
Holt, Joseph, 14, Smith street, L. B.
Holt, Mary, Manchester road
Howarth, Thomas, Bridgman street
Hasleden, ——, St. George street
Hulton Charity School, School st., Moor lane—Master: Thomas Kenyon. Mistress: Catharine Kay, r Wood street
INFANT SCHOOLS:—
Parish Church, /Churchgate.—Ann Beswick, Lane ends, Haulgh
St. John's, Foundry square.—MaryAnn Collier, r Crompton street
St George's.—Maria Robinson, r Clarence st.

Kay, Mary Elizabeth, Wood street
Latham, George. Albert place, L. B.
Lindsay, Jas., Bowkers row, r 12, Silverwell st.
Litherland, E. and M. St. George's place
Mackie, Elizabeth, 95, Bark-street
Marsden and Popplewell Charity School, Antelope court, Churchgate, (estab. 1748).—Master: Joseph Settle, r Halliwell. Mistress: Mary Torkington, r Antelope court
Methodist Schools. Fletcher street.—Master: James Raper, r Derby st., Mistress: Hannah Raper, r Derby street
Higher Bridge street.—Master: R. Harrison, r Moor lane. Mistress: Mrs. Goddart, r 11, Dale street, L. B.
Church Schools.—Cannon street, (Emanuel Church).—Master: George Betsworth. Mistress: Mary Torkington
Blackburn road, (Christ church).—Master: G. Waddington, r Blackburn street. Mistress: M. Bayley, r Derby street
Farnworth, Training.—Joseph Jenkins, Mrs. Bowker, and M. Copping
Albert place, (St. George's).—Master: Joseph Robinson, r Clarence street
Trinity square, (Trinity).—Master: James M. Rutter—Mistress: Margaret V. Rutter
Union street, (All Saints).—Master: ——
Mistress: Elizabeth Gray, Kay st.
Ogden, Edward, Blackburn street, L. B.
Roberts, Agnes, St. George's terrace
Rothwell, R. Sydney street, r 27, Foundry st
Storkey, Peter, Blackhorse street
Tootell, William, Derby street, r Crook street
United Brethren's Institute, Dean street, L. B. Manager: T. Burkitt, r 162, Kay street, do.
*Wrigley, L. higher Bridge st. r 98 Bark street

MACKIE'S
BOLTON DIRECTORY.

NOTE.—Where parties do not reside on, or by their premises, in most cases the residence is given. Where there are two or more Partners, the first residence given is that of the first partner, and so on. The figures refer to the List of Chapels and Churches, page 31. Any street, &c., will be easily found by referring to the Wards, page 29, 30, & 31.

CLERGY.

3 BAKER, Rev. Franklin, Fairfield House, Little Bolton
Barrett, Rev. John, Farnworth
Bateson, Rev. A. Egerton
14 Beaumont, Rev. M. H. Bath-st
6 Berry, Rev Thomas, James-st.
Bingham, Rev Richd. Harwood
9 Brown, Rev W.L, M A. Rosehill
Burns, Rev. William, Vicarage, Farnworth
18 CARTER, Rev. T., Pilkington-st.
15 Chamberlain, Rev. Walter, Folds road, 110.
Chambers, Rev. Mr., Halliwell,
17 Cross, Rev. John Edward, 12, Silverwell-street
Crossley, Rev. Mr , Farnworth
DYSON, Rev Joseph, Farnworth
10 & 11 EASTWOOD, Rev J. Howell Croft
21 Edwards, Rev. Charles, 52, Higher Bridge-street
4 Etheridge, Rev. Benjamin, Chorley old road
Frazer, Rev. Mr. Astley bridge
Ffolliott, Rev. W. Farnworth
GIRDLESTONE, Rev. E.. Dean
19 HADFIELD, Rev. Alfred, Victoria Terrace
Hewitt, Rev. D. Commission-st.
Hodgson, Rev. D. S, Pembroke place, Chorley new road
14 JONES, Rev. Neville, St George's Terrace
10 & 11 Kay, Rev. Robert, Higher Bridge-street
2 Leach, Rev. John, Kay-st. L. B.
7 Levy, Rev. Geo, Blackburn-st.
17 Loxam, Rev. T. St George's-ter.
5 & 8 MARSLAND, Rev. G. Derby-st.

Milton, Rev. W. Halliwell
13 Mc'Gill, Rev D. Bridgmanplace
Mc' Michael, Rev. John Clunie, Farnworth
5 & 8 Mc'Owan, Rev. J. Bridge-st.
19 NEWBY, Rev. J. Bridgman-st.
1 Nimmo, Rev. David, Bath-st.
PAGAN, Rev. S., Darcy Lever
Pope, Rev. Thos , Darcy Lever
20 Porter, Rev. Lewis, Tonge
Probert, Rev. John, Egerton
17 Richardson, Rev H. Churchgate
Richardson, Rev John, Walmsley Church, Turton
SHARP, Rev. Mr., Halliwell
Sargent, Rev W. H, Farnworth
17 Slade, Rev. James, (Vicar of Bolton, and Canon of Chester), Churchgate
6 Scott, Rev. Mr Derby-street
16 Smith, Rev. T. Palace-street, St. George's-street
Spencer, Rev. James, Chapel Town
5 & 8 Walton, Rev. Daniel, 155, Higher Bridge-street
Wheeler, Rev. Jas., Ainsworth
Woodman, Rev. W. Kersley
Wright, Rev. Charles, Belmont

GENTRY.

Ainsworth, Peter, Esq., Smithills Hall
Ashton, Mrs. Jane, St. George's street, (99)
Ashworth, Mr Edmund, Folds cottage, Smith street
Barnes, Mr George, St. George's st
Barnes, Mr J. R., Darley hall, Farnworth   [Farnworth
Barnes, Mrs. Eliza, Greenbank

Balshaw, Mr W. Rosehill cottage
Barrow, Mr J., Wellington place
Barlow, Mr Richard, Stonehill
Bearpark, Mr Thos. Tipping place
Brabin, Mrs Mary, Bath street
Blinkhorn, Mrs Susan, Bark street
Bromiley. Mrs Mary, Park hill place, Chorley old road
Badger, Mr Joseph, Newport place
Badger, Mr Richd.   do.
Bolling, Mrs Wm. Darcy Lever Hall
Bolling, Mr Edward James, Darcy Lever Hall
Brierley, Mrs Mary, Bark street
Broadbent, Mr T. Bradford place
Buckle, Miss M A. Bridgman st
Chantler, Mr Joseph, Pikes lane
Chantler, Mr Thomas, Pikes lane
Charlton, Mr F. Little Hulton
Clare, Mrs Jane, 167 Bridge street
Coe, Mr James, Newport street
Cooper, Mr Rd., St George's ter.
Cooper, Mrs Margt., Silverwell st
Crompton, Miss M St. George's st
Crompton, Mr William, High st
Cron, Miss, 141 St George's street
Crook, Mrs Ellen, 14 Bullock st
Dean, Jno. Esq., Silverwell house
Dean, Mr Adam, Goodwin house
Dean, Mrs,   do.
Eskrick, Mr John, Brownlow fold
Eskrick, Mr Henry,   do.
Fell, Mrs Elizabeth, Mount pleasant, Well street L B
Fowler, Miss Betsy, Silverwell st
Gardner, Mrs Mary, Silverwell st
Gaskell, Mrs Elizabeth, Rose place
Gill, the Misses, Newport terrace
Green, Mr Thos Manchester road
Greenwell, Mr Peter, Bridgman st
Grime, Mrs Ann, Albert place
Grundy, Mrs Maria, Blackburn st
Haigh, Mrs. Stone cottage, Higher Bridge street
Hall, Miss E. B., Acres' field
Hardman, Mrs, 27 West bank, Chorley new road
Hartley, Mr John, Summerfield
Harrison, Mr W., Rose cottage, Brinks brow
Harwood, Mrs Alice, Clarence st
Haselden, Mrs E. 138 St George's street
Haslam, Mrs Ellen, Parkhill place Chorley old road
Haslam, Miss, Lark hill
Heap, Mr John, Pembroke place
Heap, Miss, 1 Pembroke place

Heaton, Mrs Elizbth. Bridgman st
Henry, Mrs Martha, Greenhill
Hewitt, Mr David, West bank, Chorley new road
Heywood, R. Esq. Newport terrace
Hickson, Mr Peter, 85 Bark street
Higson, Mr Wm. Bridgman street
Hodgson, Mrs. 2 Pembroke place
Horrocks, Mrs Mary, 85 St Geo.'s place
Horrocks, Mr John,   do.
Howarth, Miss, 93, West bank, Chorley new road
Howarth, Mr Edm., Sharples hall
Howell, Miss, Manchester road
Howard, Mr Jno., Blackhorse st
Ingham, Mrs, 1 High street
Isherwood, Mrs E., Bridgman st
Jackson, Miss, West bank
Johnson. Mr R , Bridgman street
Johnson, the Misses, Wellington place, Manchester road
Kay, Mrs M., St. George's terrace
Kay, Mr Robt., Chorley new road
Kay, Mr John, West bank, Chorley new road
Kay, Mr J , Turton
Kearsley, Mr T., Ainsworth lodge
King, Mrs Sarah, Victoria terrace
Langshaw, Captain Edmund, 12 Silverwell street
Lee, Mr T., 81 St. George's place
Lever, the Misses, Newport terrace
Lever, Mr Thomas,   do.
Lomax, Mr, Birch hall
Lomax, Mr Johnson, Bradshawgt.
Lomax, Robert, Esq , Lomax fold Harwood
Lomax, Mrs A., 15 Silverwell st
Lord, Mrs, 109 Bark street
Lord, Mr Robert, Farnworth
Lord, Mr Joseph,   do.
Lupton, Miss Eliza, Acres' field
Makant, Mr John, Bath street
Mallett, Mrs S. 137 St George's st
Mangnall, Mrs Sarah, Bullock st.
Maugnall Mr John, Sharples
Mangnall, Mr Richard, Rosehill
Marsden, Mrs M., Bradford place,
Merry, Mrs Martha, Greenhill
Monks, Mr James, Chapel street
Morris Miss Mary, Batn street
Moss, Mr William, Rosehill
Moxon, Mr John, Silverwell st
Nuttal Miss B., 6 Park hill place
Olivant, Miss B. 14 St George's ter.
Pearson, Miss, 30 West bank
Peat, Mrs Jane, 42 Folds road

Pennington, Mr Saml. Halliwell

Plumber, Mr J., Blackburn street

Richardson, Captain James, Silverwell street

Robinson, Miss, 7 St.Geo's. terrace

Robinson, Mrs, 69 Higher Bridge street

Rostron, Mrs. Halliwell

Rothwell, Miss, 62 Higher Bridge street

Rushton, Miss Elizabeth,Wood st

Scowcroft, Mrs Alice, Mawdsley st

Sharpe, Mr Theophilus, Deane

Shakespear,Miss E., Shakspeare court, Manchester road

Sharples, Mrs, 17 Chapel street

Sharples, Mrs A., St.Geo's.terrace

Skelton, Mr Joseph,Bowker's row

Slater, the Misses, Tipping place

Smith, Mrs Mary, Bridgman st

Smith, Miss Esther, Smith street

Smith, Miss Mary Ann, Wellington place

Smith, Mr. David, Newport street

Spencer, Mr Joseph, Orlando st

Sturdy, Mrs Jane, 140 St. George's street

Taylor, Mrs, 29, Bridge street

Taylor, Miss C., St Geo's. terrace

Taylor, Mr G., Chorley new road

Thompson, Mrs S., Water st., L.B

Tong, Mr Thomas, Bradford place Manchester road

Wainhouse, the Misses, Rose place Manchester road

Walker, John, Esq,Bradford house

Walker, Mrs E., Manchester road

Walsh, Robt. Esq. Parkhill place, Chorley old road

Wallwork, Mrs R., Orlando street

Ward, Mrs, 9 St George's terrace

Watkins, Mrs F., Newport terrace

Whitehead, Mrs B., Silverwell st

Winder, Mrs M., Tipping place

Wolfenden, Mrs., 18, Silverwell st

Wood, Mr J. Reynolds, Rosehill

Wood, the Misses, West bank; house Chorley new road

Wood, Mr Thos. Chorley new road

Accountants.

Horrocks, Jas., 12, Nelson square

Mulliner & Tyrer, 16, Acres' field, *r* 141, StGeorge'sroad; Back o'th' bank

Silvester, Forrest, Crown-street

Tunnah, John, Hotel street

Wharton, George F., Acres' field

Wolfenden, J. R. Silverwell street

Agents.

See preceding list, also
Cotton Yarn Dealers, Fire and Life Office Agents, Land Agents & Surveyors.

Ayrton, Henry, Bridgman place

Baron,John,(house)Bradshawgate

Barnes, George, (Knowles&Stott) near Stoneclough.

Binks, Wm.(house)Bradshawgate

Boardman, Ralph, Ship gates

Bragg, John, Deansgate

Brown, William, (Prov. Society) Bourne street.

Burrell, John, (Mancr. Guardian) Crown street.

Crompton,Peter,(house)Dawes'st.

Dawson,George, (book)89,Kay st.

Flitcroft,Robt.(CanalCo.)*r*Church wharf.

Flitcroft, Jas. (Brocklebank) do.

Gorton, Jas., lower Bridgman st.

Greenhalgh, Geo. (general) Princess street.

Healey, John, (machine) Bark st.

Johnson, John, (Joseph Ridgway) Halliwell toll bar.

Knott, Daniel, Folds street, *r* Bradford square.

Lander, Robt.(deliverer for Blackie & Son. Publishers, Glasgow) Bark st.

Lawson, Jos.(news)Bradshawgate

Lomax, Jacob, (house) Crook st.

Liptrott, Peter, (Wine & Spirit) 5 Orlando street.

Mawdsley, John, & Son, (general) Market street.

Mackie, Alexander,GeneralAgent, 95 Bark street.—See Advertisement.

Mercer, Jas., (house) Gt. Moor st.

Padbury, Saml. (W.Hulton, Esq.) *r* Rose Cottage, Over Hulton.

Pearce, John, (Earl Balcarres) *r* Rose place, Rose hill.

Ross, Robert, (Earl Bradford) *r* Bridgman place.

Sawdon, Thos. & Co., (Darcey & Co's Dublin Porter) Bridge street.

Taylor, William, Brinks brow

Walsh, Roger, (P.Ainsworth,Esq.) Clough Cottage, Halliwell.

Winterburn, G. *(*news*)* Deansgate

Architects.

Greenhaulgh, James, Acres'-field

Nicholson, Wm., 4, Ridgway gates

Whittaker, J.W. Exchange street east, *r* Bullock street.

Artists.

Eccles, George, Black horse street

Pilkington, Wm. Taylor brow; *r* 194 Folds road

Robson, Thomas, Deansgate

BOLTON DIRECTORY.

Attornies.

Marked thus— Commissioners under the Fines and Recoveries Act; and for taking the Acknowledgements of Married Women.*

Brierley, Edward, Bowker's row

Briggs & Jackson, (Clerks to the County Magistrates and Trustees of Great Bolton) Wood street; *residences of both, Sharples.*

Brownlow, Richard, Bridge st., *r* Horwich

*Cross & Greenhalgh, Acres'-field, *r* Halliwell Lodge; 3, Bradford-terrace. Mr. Cross is also Sheriff-deputy for granting Replevins within the hundred of West Derby, Salford, Leyland, and Blackburn.

*Dawes, Matthew, Mawdsley street *r* West brook.

Gaskell, John, Mawdsley street

*Gaskell, Samuel, Churchgate; *r* Wellington Cottage, Chorley old road

Glover, Henry, Mealhouse lane, *r* St George's terrace.

Gordon, John, (*Clerk of the Peace and Clerk to Trustees of Little Bolton)* Acres'-field ; *r* Chorley new road.

Gibson, Richard, 3 StGeorge's ter.

*Haworth, Adam L, Mealhouse lane, *r* Higher Dunscar, Turton.

Haworth, William, do. do.

Haworth, Edmund, junr., Exchange street east, *r* Chorley new road

Hibbert, Robert Andrew, Wood street, *r* Breightmet.

Holden, Taylor, and Andrews, Acres'-field ; *r* Summerfield ; Ainsworth Hall ; Rose hill. Mr. Holden is also Clerk to County Court, and Mr. Taylor Borough Coroner.

Hulton, John, Bowker's row; *r* Bridgman-place.

Jardine, Thomas, Bradshawgate, *r* 11, St George's terrace.

Knowles, Jas. ('Town Clerk) Acres' field, *r* Bradford terrace.

Langshaw, Edmund, (*Clerk to the County Magistrates,)* 12, Silverwell st.

Richardson and Marsland, Acres' field ; *r* Folds, 112 ; Bridge street

Rushton and Armitstead, Acres' field; *r* West Bank; Halliwell Cottage

Salt, John, Bow street

*Watkins, Jas. K. (Clerk to Turton Reservoir Committee ; Clerk to the Ratcliffe, Bolton and St Helens, Boland Westhoughton, Turnpike Road Trusts ; Clerk to the Committee of Assessed, & Property & Income Taxes for Bolton district ; Clerk to Mather's Charity ; Secretary to the Governors of Bolton Grammar School.)—Wood street, *r* Haulgh Cottage.

Whittam, James, Dixon Green,

Winder and Broadbent, (*Agents for the Property Protection Society)* Bowker's row; *residen:* Tonge Moor; Sunny bank, Haulgh. Mr. Winder is also Clerk to the Borough Magistrates.

*Woodhouse, John, (*Clerk to the Board of Guardians ; Superintendent Registrar of Births, &c.)* Acres' field, *r* Greenfield.

Young, Thomas, Bridge street, *r* Blackburn street.

Auctioneers and Appraisers.

Brierley, Thomas, Newport street

Brierley, Henry, Exchange st.west

Entwisle, Roger, do. east

Greenhalgh, George, Princess st.

Hayhurst, William, Market street

Lomax, Wm. & Sons, Acres'-field

Lomax,William, jun. Exchange st east, *r* Mawdsley street.—*See Advert.*

Parkinson, James, Cheapside

Baby-Linen Warehouse.

Binks, Mrs. Milliner&Dressmaker *See Advertisement*

Bankers.

(See Banks in Almanack, page 2.)

Jas. Cross, Esq., Halliwell Lodge

Peter Ormrod, Esq. Chamber hall

Robert Barlow, Esq. Snow hill

Thomas Lever Rushton, Esq. West Bank.

Thomas Appleton, Esq. Egerton *Messrs. Hardcastle & Co's Bank.*

Bank of Bolton; Joint-Stock. *List of Partners may be had at the Stamp Office, price 10s. 6d.*

Bakers and Flour Dealers.
(See also Corn Dealers.)

Barnes, Thomas, Derby street

Barrett, Peter, Bradshawgate

Bateson, Benjamin, Kay street

Bowen, John, Folds road

Bradley, James, Black horse street

Byers, Robert, Bradshawgate

Doodson, H.Bamber's court,D'gate

Evans, Thomas, Oxford street

Foster, Peter, Market place; *r* Breightmet

Greenhalgh, Richard, Lever street

Harwood, Robert, Deansgate

Hayward, John, Churchgate

Healey, Elijah, Lever street

Horrocks, Henry, Deansgate

Houghton, John, Cheapside

Knowles, John & James, Market place and Derby street.

Large, Thomas Gilbert,Churchgate

Lee, Thomas, Newport street

39

Lomax, Arthur, Hotel street
Lomax, Rothwell, Manor street
Marshall, G. Brinks brow
Marsh, Samuel, Mill hill
Ormrod, Joseph, Cheapside
Ormrod, Samuel, Barnes street
Pearson, John, Kay street
Pilkington, James, Bradshawgate
Pitfield, Charles, Great Moor st.
Rothwell, N. Churchgate
Scowcroft, Thomas, Bradshawgate
Turner, James, Deansgate
Wigglesworth, Thomas, Deansgate

Basket and Skip Makers.
Abbatt, Benjamin, Market street and Deansgate.
Best, James, Bowker's row and Oxford street.
Hargreaves, Rd., Bradshawgate
Mortimer, George, Newport street
Thistlethwaite, Wm. Market place, r 47 Bradshawgate

Beersellers.
Ainscow, Susanna, Moor lane
Ashton, William, Crook street
Atkinson, William, Chorley street
Atherton, Robert, Kay street
Bates, Nancy, Crook street
Boardman, Major, Moor lane
Boardman, Samuel, Bow street
Bogle, George, Folds road
Bolton, Mary, Bridgeman place
Booth, Luke, Mill hill
Bridge, John, Old acres
Brandwood, John, Hulme street
Barrett, M., Bradshawgate
Bullough, B., Higher bridge street
Burton, Ruth, Pike's lane
Clegg, Abraham, Kay street
Cox, J., Chorley street
Crighton, Thomas, Weston street
Crompton, John, Bridge street
Crompton, John, Daubhill
Crowther, James, Bradshawgate
Dewhurst, John, Blackburn street
Dobson, Mary, Wood street, L.B
Drury, Robert, Dean street
Dugelby, Thomas, Kay street
Entwisle, James, Mill hill
Entwisle, W. A. Ashburner street
Fielding, James, Higher bridge st
Fishwick, Betty, do. do.
Fletcher, William, Kay street
Flintoff, Robert, Newport street
Garthside, Mary, Bridgman place
Gent, Henry, Bradshawgate
Gerrard, Joseph, Pike's lane

Graham, Joseph, Kay street
Greenhalgh, Robert, Manor street
Greenhalgh, James, Pike's lane
Green, Thomas, Brinks brow
Gregson, N. Water street
Grime, Robert, Kay street
Hamer, Robert, Crook street
Hartley, William, Kay street
Harwood, Edmund, Trinity street
Healey, Alice, Moor lane
Heyes, Nicholas, Union buildings
Hill, John, Mill hill
Hilton, Simon, Garside street
Hilton, William, Bradshawgate
Hilton, William, Moor lane
Holt, Thomas, Moor lane
Horrocks, Joseph, Moor lane
Horrocks, James, Union street
Howarth, Philip, Kay street
Howarth, Alice, Blackburn st. L.B.
Hoyle, John, do. do.
Hall, John, Turton street
Hurst, William, Chorley street
Hutchinson, Margaret, Bow st.
Hyde, Thomas, Folds street
Johnson, James, Bradshawgate
Johnson, Thomas, Nelson square
Johnson, Thomas, Union street
Johnson, John, Brinks brow
Kay, Henry, Blackburn street
Kay, James, Mill street
Kay, Mary, Mill street
Kearsley, Edward, Pike's lane
Kirkman, Robert, Trinity street
Knowles, Thomas, Kay street
Kussley, Robert, Bradshawgate
Latham, E., Mort field
Lawson, Thomas, Moor lane
Lawson, Elizabeth, Great Moor st
Lee, James, Tipping place
Lee, John, Union street
Lever, Thomas, Crook street
Liptrot, Thomas, Chorley street
Lomax, John, Great Moor street
Lomas, Robert, Hotel street
Long, William, Pike's lane
Long, John, Great Moor street
Marsden, John, Burton street
Mason, Robert, Bradshawgate
Massey, Jane, Great Moor street
Mather, Charles, Kay street
Metcalfe, John, Charles street
Mitchell, William, Barn street
Moscrop, John, Great Moor street
Morris, John, Weston street
Morris, Charles, Moor lane
Nuttal, John, Great Moor street

Nuttal, Thomas, Chorley street
Orrell, Henry, Union buildings
Parkinson, William, Folds road
Parker, Richard, Chorley street
Parr, Richard, Moor lane
Peat, David, Weston street
Pilkington, Richard, Gilnow st
Poole, Henry, Cross street
Rigby, Benjamin, Falcon street
Rostron, Abraham, Smith street
Roberts, Thomas, Folds road
Rothwell, Richard, Bull field
Rook, Andrew, Newport street
Scowcroft, David, Mill street
Seddon, John, Blackburn st., L.B
Seddon, John, Nelson street
Seddon, John, Trinity street
Seddon, Henry, Bradshawgate
Settle, John, Halliwell road
Schofield, Margeret, Newport st
Sharples, James, Churchgate
Silcock, Ann, Rumworth
Smith, Samuel, Moor lane
Smith, John, Church street
Stansfield, David, Spaw lane
Sutcliffe, Wright, Crook street
Sugden, James, Trinity street
Taylor, Henry, Great Moor street
Thompson, John, Moor lane
Thornley, John, Crook street
Thornton, Thomas Mill hill
Urmston, John, Crook street
Wallwork, Joseph, Gas house street
Warburton, Thomas, Kay street
Walsh, John, Chorley street
Whittaker, Robert, Great Moor st
Whitehead, Joseph, Folds road
Wood, John, Great Moor street
Wordall, B., Folds road

Blacking Manufacturers.
Briggs, R. Middle street
Margerson, John, Grime street
Pilling, John, Derby street

Blacksmiths.
Marked ‡ are also Wheelwrights—See also Wheelwrights.
‡Almond & Norris, Bradshawgate, r Cheapside; Sweet Green.
‡Baxter, John, Little Hulton
‡Boardman, Thomas, Ainsworth
Bridge, James, Tonge
‡Bradley, Thomas, Deane
‡Burgess, John, Sharples
‡Burgess, Joseph, do.
Crook, John, back Crown street
Crook, Edward, (bell hanger) Taylor brow; r back Crown street.

‡Dutton, Rich. 101 St George's st.
‡Fowler, Luke, Knowsley street
Gerrard, Thomas, Deane
Higson, Hen. (bell hanger) Bridge st
Hollingworth, William, Derby st.
Hope, Farnworth, Over Hulton
Howarth, Robert, Farnworth
Leigh, Henry, Blackburn st. L.B:
Lomax, John, Queen street
Pearson, Henry, Derby street
‡Prescott, James, Bridge street
Riley, John, Church wharf
Riley, William, Derby street
Vose, Ralph, Halliwell road
Walsh, Jas., Queen st. Farnworth
Walsh, John, Nan lane, do.
Walsh, Robert, do.
Wharton, George, (horse shoeing) Chancery lane.
Worsley, Henry, White Lion brow

Bleachers.
Ainsworth, R., Son & Co., Halliwell; r Moss bank.
Blair & Sumner, Mill hill; r Mill hill house; 115 The Folds.
Bradshaw Works Co., Bradshaw; John Cross, resid. Partner, Bradshaw
Bridson, Ridgway, Son and Co., Chorley street, L.B., and Lever bank. Warehouse, 6 College land, St Mary's Gate, Manchester; r Bridge house; Vale bank
Cartwright, John, & Co. Turton
Chadwick, James, & Bro., Eagley Mills, Sharples; 59 Church st., Mancr.
Cross, Thomas, Mortfield
Eden & Thwaites, Astley bridge, Sharples.
Hardcastle, James, Firwood, Tonge
Heys, Joseph, Burnden; 41 Dickenson street, Manchester.
Hollins, Ed., & Co., Breightmet
Horridge, T. G. R., Great Lever
Knowles, Talbot, Tonge
Longworth, Wm & Co., Springfield, Turton.
Seddon, John, Breightmet
Slater, George & James, Dunscar
Slater, John, & Co. Back o'th'bank
Smith, John, jun., & Co., Gt. Lever
Williams, Thomas, Ainsworth

Bobbin Turner and Skewer Maker.
Hart, John, Cannon st. r Derby st

Boarding Houses.
Brown, Eliza, 8 Nelson square
Lindsay, James, 12, Silverwell st
Sharples, Ann, St George's terrace

Boiler & Gasometer Makers.
(See also Engineers and Millwrights.)

Hall, Samuel, Lever street
Latham, Dan Wood, (Vulcan Foundry) Foundry st, r Wellington place

Bookkeepers and Cashiers.

Ainsworth, *Samuel*, 9 Bullock street
Badder, Richard, higher Bridge st
Bamber, John, Haigh hall
Barber, David, Sidney street
Bardsley, Barnett, Gilnow
Beswick, Charles, 63 Newport st.
Blunt, M. Belmont
Bradshaw, Joshua, Waterloo st.
Bradley, John, Turton street
Bridge, William, Derby street
Briggs, Charles, Bridgman place
Broadbent, Thomas, 52 Bullock st
Bolton, J. Belmont
Crowshaw, James, Rose hill
Davies, Joseph, 13 High street
Dixon, Evan, Foundry street
Entwisle William, Green hill
Fell, George, Green street
Fletcher, Abm., Back o'th' bank
Fogg, James, Bradshawgate
Foster, Edward, Crook street
Foster, William, Bath street
Gerrard, Joseph, 173 Blackburn st
Glaister, T., junr., 141 Folds road
Gordon, Peter, Rosehill
Greenhalgh, John, Rosehill
Grenhalgh, Robert Yates, Mill hill place
Hardman, John, Lever street, L. B.
Hart, William, Bow street
Harrison, Richard, York street
Haslam, P., St. Helena
Hindley, James, 60, Higher bridge street
Hope, Thomas, Mill hill place
Inman, John, St. George's terrace
Isherwood, Abraham, Back lane
Jackson, William, Canal Wharf
Johnson, Thomas, Nelson square,
Kay, William, Lever street
Lee, Jno. Hampson, Clarence street
Litherland, W. St. George's place
Lomax, Thomas, Kirkhall cottage Chorley old road
Lomax, John, Barn street
Makin, John, 4 Blackburn street
Makin, Wm. P., 4 Blackburn st.
Mangnall, James, Haigh street
Milne, John, Market street
Mitchell, J, jun., Falcon street
Morris, James, Bank street
Moscrop, Thomas, Folds road

Nurse, George, New Market place
Parnell, William, 71 Back lane
Phethean, John, Moor lane
Poole, Henry, Cross street
Ramsbottom, John, Bridgeman st.
Reynolds, John, Folds road
Rivett, John, Farnworth
Rostron, Major, Cockerill spring
Rothwell, Peter, Garside street
Rushton, Robert, Commission st.
Smith, John, Derby street
Smith, Peter, Derby street
Smith, Robert, Bullock street
Stokes, Robert, 10 Tanners hole
Taylor, John, 26 Falcon street
Thistlethwaite, Anthony, Kestor cottage
Thornley, William, Derby street
Tootell, William, Great Moor st
Unsworth, John, Derby street
Unsworth, Timothy, 6 North place Foundry street
Walsh, John, Bath street
Whowell, John, High street
Wilson, John, Bridgman place
Wolfenden, Charles Silverwell st
Wood, Dan, 7 Bullock street
Yates, Thomas, 2 Princess street
Yates, James, Kay street

Booksellers, Bookbinders, and Printers.

Those marked thus* are Bookbinders only; those marked thus † are Printers only.

Bradbury, Henry, Deansgate, r Bark street
† Bridge, Wm., (Chronicle Office) r Derby street
Gardner, Samuel, Bradshawgate, r Wood street
Gowland, M., Bow st., Bookseller
Hargreaves, James, Folds street
Haslam, John & Son, Exchange street, West, Booksellers
Heaton, John, Stamp Office, Deansgate, r Bradford terrace
Holden, R. M. Mealhouse lane, r St. George's terrace
† Kenyon, Robert, Oxford street
† Morris, Thomas, Oxford street
Ogle, John, Market st, r Green hill
Roberts, Thomas, Bradshawgate
* Scholes, J., Watson's Shambles,
† Staton, James, Exchange street, East, r 43, Newport street
Taylor, Samuel, Farnworth
Whowell, Robert, Barn street
Winterburn, George, Bookseller, Deansgate, r Ridgway gates

Boot & Shoe Makers.

Asquith, John, Prestolee
Atherton, John, Weston street
Atherton, Joseph, Sidney street
Austin & Son, Corner of Bridge st. Deansgate
Aynscough, J. 60 Cross street, L.B.
Baldwin, Richard, Spring gardens
Baron, John, 83 Folds road
Baron, James, Moor lane
Barton, William, Green street
Bell, Joseph, 28 Crown street
Beswick, Thomas, Churchgate
Black, J., & J. P. Beswick, Deansgate, near Oxford street
Blore, Cooper, Blackburn st., L.B.
Boardman, & Co., Darcy Lever
Booth, Richard, Halliwell
Bowden, Luke, Farnworth
Bradbury, John, Grime street
Brogden, J. 59 Black Horse street
Bromilow, William, Bank street
Bromilow, Abraham, Green street
Bromley, Walter, 161 Deansgate
Bromley, George, 55 Weston street
Brown, Jas,(& Clogger) Deansgate
Brown, John, Churchgate
Calderbank, William, Folds road
Carrodus, James, Bradshawgate
Chapman, Edward, Prestolee
Chorlton, William, Kearsley
Clarence, Peter, King street
Clark, Richard, 20 Bank street
Clegg, John, Deansgate, near Duke's Alley
Cook, M. & E. (Shoe Warehouse) Bank street
Cunliffe, Robert, Bridgman street
Cupitt, Thomas, Old hall street
Davidson, John, 9 Blackhorse st.
Dixon, Thomas, Kearsley
Dutton, John, Deansgate
Enright, J. 81 Howell croft
Entwisle, James, Spring gardens
Fitton, R., Newport street
Flynn, Daniel, Deansgate
Friar, Francis, Prestolee
Gregory, Richard, Bridgman street
Hall, William, Ashburner street
Hardman, B. Moorlane
Harding, John, Farnworth
Haslam, William, Ridgway gates
Heaton, James, Barn street
Hesketh, John, Newport street
Higginson, R., 89 Bridge street
Hilton,James, Bradshawgate
Holding, William, All Saints st.
Holt, Robert, Bradshawgate

Hudson, W. & Son, 13. Manor st.
Hughes, William, Bradshawgate
Jackson, William, Folds road
Jones, John, Farnworth
Jones, Robert, Halliwell
Knott, George, Manor street
Lyon, George, (& Clog) Deansgate
Makinson, John, Bradshawgate
Marchant, William, Deansgate
Mather, Hulton, Little Lever
Mercer, Richard, Union street
Mitchell, James, Hotel street
M'c Cormick, James, King street Farnworth
Mc' Cormack, John, Old acres
Moffet, Robert, Barnes street
Moss, Thomas, Carey street
Mulliner, Thomas, jun., Market st See Advertisement
Nelson, Andrew, Bradshawgate
Nuttal, Thomas, Newport street
Orrel, Peter, Weston street
Pilling, James, Little Lever
Pirkins, John, Howell croft
Platt, William, Lever street
Potts, Samuel, Blackburn street
Richard, William, Howell croft
Rockliffe, Jeremiah, Brown street
Sandham, Wm., 70 Chapel street
Sharples, William, Lever street
Stephens, Thomas, Garside street
Shone, William, Bridgman street
Sykes, William, Union street
Taylor, Matthew, 2 Hulme street
Tector, Wm. Howell croft
Townley, Doctor, Charles street
Townley. Michael, 82 Bark street
Walsh, Thomas, Crook street
Wareing, William, Manor street
Wharton, James, Bradshawgate
Wilkinson, John, Bradshawgate
Woodruffe, William, Deansgate
Wright, J., Brown street
Wynne, H., Deansgate

Brass Founders.

(See also. Brass and Iron Founders.)
Green, Richard, Taylor field, r Brinks brow
Parkinson, Thomas, Newport st.
Taylor and Galloway, Moor lane r Mawdsley street; r 50 Back lane

Braziers & Tin Plate Workers

Berry, James, Darley st. Farnworth
Brown, Joseph, Churchgate
Brotherton, Thomas, Bradshawgt.
Hind William, Newport street

Holt, Robert, Folds road
Marshall, Cornelius, Manor street, r 3 Bow street
Moss, Robert, Deansgate
Parkinson, Thomas, Newport street
Robson, George, Deansgate
Sherlock, Hugh, Moor lane
Twisse, Peter, Wharf street
Unsworth, George, Kearsley
Warburton, John, Kearsley
Winder, Robert, Moor lane
Wilson. James, Crown street
Wood, Ellis, Bank street

Brewers.

Newstead & Walker, Bradshawgt.
Nightingale, R. & T., 138 Kay st.
Lever, Thomas, Crook street
Sawdon, T. & Co., 134 Bridge st.
Young, Sarah, and Son, 53 All Saints' street

Brickmakers.

Dean, John, Lever street, r Silverwell house
Greenwood, E. & A., Kearsley
Hardcastle, John, Fletcher street r Woolpack, Deansgate
Jones, John, Blackburn street
Marsden, Jas. & Joseph, Lever st.
Mesdale, James, Lever street
Ormrod, Thomas, Lever street

Bricklayers.

Bolton, James, Deansgate
Brown, Thomas, Kearsley
Brown, L. Chorley street
Flitcroft, Joseph, Derby street
Jones, John, Blackburn street
Lee, John, Kay street
Shaw, John, Water street
Shaw, T. Moor lane
Shaw. Joseph, St. George's road
Stirrup, James, Newport street—

Brushmakers.

Best, James, (& Skip Maker) Oxford street
Carling, Richard, Back Cheapside See Advertisement
Cocker, Jno. Cheapside, see Advr.
Hadfield, Richard, Moor lane
Jones, Frederick, Ashburner street
Jones, Sarah, Great Moor street
Wilkinson, & Warburton, Deansgate, r Greenhill r Deansgate
Winward, William. Newport st.
Young, James, Ashburner street
Young, James, Howell croft

Builders.

(See Stonemasons, Timber Merchants, and Builders.)

Butchers.

Adamson, Richard, Derby street
Anderson, Robert, sen. Deansgate
Anderson, Robt..jun. Howell croft
Birtwisle, Joseph, Deansgate
Birtwisle, Henry, Deansgate
Briercliffe, William, Newport st
Briercliffe, Thomas, Manor street
Butler, Robert, Kearsley
Charnley, John, Churchgate
Child, William, Crook street
Cordingly, J. Bridgman street
Crompton, John, Farnworth
Crompton, Peter, Oxford street
Crosdale, Henry, Derby street
Dickinson, John, Bridgman street
Fairclough, Ellen, Edgworth
Forrest, John, John street
Garthside, James, Kearsley
Halliwell, Thomas, Churchgate
Hargreaves, Richard, Moor lane
Harper, William, Deansgate
Hartley, Thomas, Hulme street
Haslam, Jonth., (Pork)Deansgate
Haslam, James, (Pork) Cross Axe entry
Hilton, John, Derby street
Hodson, Peter, Derby street
Horan, Stph. (Pork) Cheapside
Jackson, J., Nan lane, Farnworth
Kay, Ralph, (Pork) New Market place
Kemp, William, Bridge street
Kearsley, Mary, Blackburn street
Lever, Thomas, Moor lane
Manchester, John, Deansgate
Melling, William, Folds road
Monks, James, 3 Weston street
Parkinson, Edmund, Dixon green
Patterson. Richard, Deansgate
Rigby, James, Farnworth,
Scholes Robert, Turton street
Scholes, William, Bradshawgate
Shackleton, Jonth., Bradshawgate
Scowcroft, Alfred, Churchgate
Shuttleworth, John, Chapel street
Steele, J. J., (Pork) Bradshawgate
Taylor, Samuel, Market street
Thwaites, William, Bradshawgate
Vickers, John, 176 Folds road
Walmsley, T. Blackburn st., L.B.
Wilkinson, Henry, 140 Kay street
Wolstenholme. James, Manor st.

Cabinet Makers

*Marked thus * are also Upholsterers.*

Brierley, Thomas, Newport-street
*Charnley, Richard, 6, All Saints'-st.
Crackston, Thomas, Great Moor-str.
*Dorning, Jonathon, Bradshawgate
*Fryer, Ralph, 206, Folds road
Garnett, J. Deansgate, r Duke's Alley
Gooden, James, Deansgate
Graham, Thomas, 31, Bridge street
*Green, J. & W. New Market place
Harwood, Richard, (House decorator see advertisement), Bradshawgate
Hartley, William, 72, Bridge street
Higson, William, Newport street
Leigh, William, Oxford street
Metcalfe, James, Crown street
Santley, Joseph, Mealhouse lane
Wilson, R., 139, Bridge street

Calicoe Printers.

Bradshaw Works Co., John Cross, Esq., resident partner, Bradshaw Hall
Millington, George, Edgeworth
Roberts, John, Prestolee
Williams, Thomas, Ainsworth

Carriage Owners—*for hire.*

Greenwood & Higson, Bridge street
Greenwood, John, Bradshawgate, r Pendleton.

Cart Sheet Tarpauling Manufacturers.

Bolton, Thomas, Well street, L.B.
Borsay, James, Oxford street, r Howel croft.
Flitcroft, James, Black Horse street
Flitcroft, Thomas, Market street
Huworth, John, Hotel street, r 12 Derby street.

Carvers and Gilders.

Masper, Augustine, Churchgate (See advertisement).
Rothwell, Edward, Bradshawgate
Tilling, Edward, Bradshawgate

Chair Makers

Brotherton, *William,* Crown street
Hyde, *Peter,* Ashburner street
Leigh, *Richard,* Oxford street, r Velvet walks.
Leigh, William, Oxford street
Morris, John, Exchange street west, r. Duke's Alley.
Morris, Peter, Duke's Alley

Cheese Mongers

Mark thus * attend on Mondays only.

Challinor, Ralph, Deansgate
Cunliffe, James, 2 Market street, r Manor street
Dixon, Thomas, 10 Deansgate, r Preston.
*Entwisle, John, 156 Deansgate, r Barn street
*Entwisle, Thomas, Deansgate, r Greenhill

Howcroft, Isaac, Crown street, r West cottage, L.B.
Latham, Richard, Deansgate, r Lostock.
*Livsey, Joseph, Meal house lane, r Preston
Markland, Richard, Cross Axe Entry, r Breightmet
Sharples and Tunnah, 9 Hotel str.
Thornton, Thomas, Old Hall street
*Toulmin, John, Deansgate, r Pres.
Whitehead, Jonathon, Deansgate,

Chemists and Druggists.

Aspinwall, W. & J. 163 Deansgate
Bamber, Alexander, Newport str.
Bullivant, James O., Bridge street
Challinor John, Moor lane
Dutton, George, New Market place
Forbes, James W., 7 Newport street
Goodwin, James. Kearsley
Gooden, Robert, 89 Deansgate
Green, George, Market place
Hart, W. & J. White Lion brow
Jackson, John, G. Moor st. (corner)
La French, George, (for the Queen) Cheapside
Lawton, Robert. Farnworth
Mc Millan John, Churchgate
Morris, James, Deansgate 151 and 152, r Chorley New road
Moscrop, Thomas, 21 Barnes street, and 179 Folds road, r Parkhill
Reynolds, Richard, Hotel street, r Halliwell
Scott, John, Farnworth
Scowcroft, James, 159 Deansgate
Scowcroft, John, 3, Deansgate
Simpson, J. R., 144 Deansgate
Taylor, Joseph, Little Lever
Warburton, James, Farnworth
Warburton, Thomas, Bradshawgate, and Church street, Atherton, (*See advertisement*)
Watson, Henry, Brown street L.B.
Watson, John, 24 Manor street
Watson, Abraham, (and Surgeon) Deansgate

Chemist—Manufacturing.

Ashton, John, Worsley road, Farnwth
Blair, Harrison, & Co., Kersley
Cross, Thomas, Farnworth
Haslam and Howarth, Burnden, r Newport place, r Little Burnden
Smith, John and Co., Great Lever
Wilson, Edward, Prestolee

Church Furniture Maker and Undertaker.

French, Gilbert James, Undertaker, Bradshawgate

Clog and Patten Makers.

Aspden, James, Blackburn street
Agar, John, 33, Ashburner street
Barlow, Richard, Bradshawgate
Bell, George, Deansgate
Bell, John, 24 Ashburner street

Berry, J., Blackburn street, L.B.
Berry, John, Farnworth
Birchby, Robert, Bradshawgate
Brockbank, George, Folds road
Brockbank, Miles, Kay street, L.B.
Bromiley, Hamer, Bridgman street
Brown, James, Deansgate
Bradshaw, George, Hulme street L.B
Callond, Thomas, 13 Kay street L.B
Cattral, J., Green street, L.B.
Cleave, C., Back Lever street, L.B.
Clegg, Noah, Lever street
Crompton, John, Newport street
Darbyshire, Isaac, Nan lane, Farnworth
Dawson, Robert, Kearsley
Emmett, J., Pitt street
Fielding, William, Deansgate
Fogg, Edward, Foundry street
Fogg, Edward, Vulcan street
Glasby, John, Darcy Lever
Gradwell, Thomas, Blackburn street
Grundy, Richard, Little Lever
Green, John, Chorley street, L.B.
Grange, L., Moor lane
Hamer, Bromilow, Bridgman street
Hancock, William, Green street
Heaton, James, Blackburn street
Hilton, James, Bradshawgate
Hilton, J., Folds road
Hilton, William, Weston street
Horrobin, J., Blackburn street, L.B.
Hughes, William, Kay-street, L.B.
Isherwood, James, Bradshawgate
Jackson, Samuel, Farnworth
Kellett, Robert, Deansgate
Kerr, Joseph, Ashburner street
Kirkman, Joseph, Ainsworth
Kirkman, Robert, Kersley
Leech, Ralph, Oxford street
Lomax, John, Churchgate
Lomax, William, Bradshawgate
Lowe, Hannah, 8 and 9 Bridge street
Mann, George, Derby street
Mellor, Richard, Derby street
Mercer, James, Deansgate and Great Moor street
Middleton, Thomas, Dixon green
Middleton, Thomas, Derby street
Morgan, John, Howell croft
Mort, Adam, Bridgman street
Muir, Archibald, Moor lane
Nuttall, Thomas, Kersley
Orrell, Joseph, 13, Union street, L.B
Parkinson, J., Turton street
Pickering, William, Independent str.
Rothwell, Peter, Little Leve
Roscoe, Mary, Darcy lever
Soncock, Henry, Folds road
Stone, Henry, Kersley
Sumner, James, Ainsworth
Tattersall, Parkinson, Bradshaw-gate
Thirlwind, William, 161, Kay st., L.B
Tomlinson, Thomas, Derby street
Tomlinson, Thomas, Shaw street

Threlfall, A., Blackburn street, L.B
Vorse, H., Hulme street, L.B
Walker, Richard, Great Moor str.
Walls, John, Blackburn street
Webster, Richard, Churchgate
Whitehead, Robert, Blackburn street
Wylde, J., Blackburn street L.B

Clothes Dealers.

Baron, J., King street
Fay, John, Deansgate
Hardman, Edward, King street
Heaton, Catherine, Deansgate
Mc Coy, Richard, Deansgate

Coach Builders.

Cooper, Joseph, Bradshawgate
Parr, James, Bradshawgate
Roberts, Brothers, Nelson square *r* Bradshawgate

Coal Dealers.

Hamer, S., Bridge street
Lowe, Isaac, Bridge street
Ormrod, William, Ashburner street *r* Pike's lane
Richards, John, 48 Derby street

Circulating Libraries.

Ainsworth, James, Horrocks street
Gardner, Samuel, Bradshawgate
Gowland, Margaret, Bow street
Gray, Amelia, Newport street
Mechanics' Institute, Bridge street
Parkinson, George, Bridge street
Reference Library, Sunday School Institute, Acres' field

Coal Merchants and Coal Owners.

Bradford, the Earl of, Orlando st.
Balcarres, the Earl of, Johnson street *r* Haigh Hall; John Pearce, Agent, Rose place, Rose hill
Charlton, Francis, Little Hulton
Darcy Lever Coal Company, Darcy Lever
Fletcher, Thomas, Little Lever
Gibson, John and Co., Little Hulton
Hulton, William, Esq., Great Moor street, *r* Over Hulton; Samuel Fadbury, Agent, *r* Rose cottage, Over Hulton
Knowles and Sons, Canal Wharf, *r* Mr. John at Little Lever, Mr. James at Astley bank
Knowles and Stott, Johnson street, *r* Mr. Stott, the Mount, near Stoneclough; Mr. George Barnes, Agent, Stoneclough
Ridgway, Joseph, Johnson street, *r* Kent; John Johnson, Halliwell Toll Bar, Agent.
Scowcroft and Brothers, Burnden, *r* Rose hill
Scowcroft and Longworth, Halliwell
Urmston, Robert, Street gate, Farnworth

Comb Makers.

Hulme, James, Deansgate
Lyons, William, Moor lane, r Howell croft
Wright, William, Old acres,' r Makinson street

Confectioners and Pastry Cooks.

Briercliffe, S. 16 Manor street L B
Chatterton, Elizabeth, Market str.
Crompton, Edward, Churchgate
Crossley, John, Turton street, L.B.
Ellis, Elizabeth, Market street
Haslam, J. & Son, Exchange street
Harwood, John, Churchgate
Holden, James, Bradshawgate
Jones, William, Mealhouse lane
Morley, James, Folds road
Norris, Margaret and Ellen, Bradshawgate
Parr, A., Bradshawgate
Ridgway, Samuel, Princess street
Wignal, John, 20 Manor street, L.B

Coopers.

Grundy, William, Exchange street west, r Lever street, L.B.
Jones, Edward, Great Moor street
Milligan, William, Newport street (See advertisement)
Ward, Elizabeth, Deansgate
Wilkinson, A. and S., Deansgate

Cork Cutter.

Cox, Daniel, Acres' field

Corn and Flour Dealers.

Marked thus * attend on Mondays only.

*Banks, Samuel, Market street, r Leigh
Barret, Peter, Bradshawgate
Binks, George, Mealhouse lane, r 170 Higher Bridge street
*Bolton, John, Market street, Harwood lee
Bradshaw, Elizabeth, Deansgate
Cunliffe, James, 2 Market street Manor street
Evans, Thomas, Oxford street
Grime, William, Bradshawgate
Haddock, Thomas and James, Oxford street, r 18 St. George's terrace r Lower Bridgman street
Hall, Richard, Bank street
Harwood, John, Deansgate, r Lower Bridgman street
Horrocks, John, Nag's head yard, Deansgate, r Back o'th' bank
Lee, William, Knowsley street
Leicester, John, Oxford street
Lever, William, Mealhouse lane, r Independent street
Lord, Ann, 5 Market street, r Bark st
Marsden, R. and T., Cheapside
Mason, John, Nag's Head yard, Sharples
Nuttall, Philip, Cheapside
Ormrod, Joseph, Cheapside

Ormrod, Peter, Bank street
*Ormrod, George, Market street
Pilkington, James, Bradshawgate
Taylor, William, Deansgate
Thompson, John, Market street, r Market square
Whitehead, Jonathon and Sons, Market street, r 7 Knowsley street
Wood, Samuel, Nag's Head yard, r Turton
Wood, James, Newport street, r Sydney street
Wood, Joseph, Market street, r Bark street
Young, John, Oxford street, r Pike's lane

Cotton Spinners.

Marked thus * are also Manufacturers.

Ainsworth and Crompton, Foundry street, L.B, r The Thorns, r Astley bank
Arrowsmith and Son, Lever street Mill, r Victoria terrace, r Victoria terrace
*Ashworth, Henry and Edmund, Turton ; Warehouse, Folds street, r The Oaks, r Egerton Hall, Turton
Balshaw, Edmund, Grime street
*Barnes, Thomas, Farnworth
Barret, Thomas and Son, Prestolee
Baxter, William, Taylor fold, r Cheapside
Bayley, J. and J. Pinfold factory, L.B
Blair and Burton, Folds road
Bleakley, James, Phoenix Mill, Little Lever, r Head o'th' lane
Bolling, Edward and William, Howel croft, Mr. E's r Silverwell street and Crompton fold
Bromley, John, Brinks brow
Burton, Thomas and Richard, Ainsworth mill
Cannon and Haslam Spaw lane and Halliwell, r Park hill, r Lark hill
Crompton, T. B., Prestolee and 3 Church street, Manchester
*Crook, Joshua and Sons, Blackburn st
*Cross, John, Lever street
*Cross, Thomas and Sons, Farnworth
Cullen, Thomas, Bow street, r West cottage, Chorley road
Cunliffe, George and Son, Mawdsley street and Byng street
Dearden Oliver, Dawson lane, r Mawdsley street
Dobson and Reeve, Black Horse street, r Blackburn street, L.B., r Dawson lane
Gardner and Bazley, Dean Mills
Gray, William and Son, Damside, r Wheatfield, Haulgh
Greenhalgh and Murton, Sharples
Gregson and Leeming, High street, r Moor lane, r 52 Derby street
*Hacking, William and John, Farnwth.
Haigh. Abraham and Son, Higher Bridge street
Hampson, William and Son, Breightmet
*Hargreaves, J. G. and C. Bridgman street, r May field, r Birch house, r Rose hill
Hindley and Lawton, Nan lane, Farnwth

Hollins, Henry, Jun., Lever street, r Rose hill

Holden, James, Undershore

Horrocks and Dearden, Queen street, Farnworth

Hughes, Amelia, Long causeway, Farnworth

Knowles, Robert, Sen., Round hill mills, Turton street, r Round hill house

Knowles, Robert, Jun., Round hill mills r Green hill

Knowles, John and George, Turton str. r 148 St George's street, r No. 100 Folds

Martin, William and Son, Fletcher st. r Newport square and Rivington

Ormrod and Hardcastle, Weston street, r Mr. P. Ormrod, Chamber hall, r Mr. James Crmrod. Halliwell lodge

Prestwich, John, Farnworth

Rothwell and Kitts, Blackhorse street, r Mr Kitts, Dean

Rylands and Sons, Ainsworth

Settle, Jonathon, Howell croft

Shuttleworth and Horrocks, Bradshaw

Skinner, David, White Lion brow, r St George's road

Slade, William, Howell croft, r Crompton fold

Smith and Bell, Bury street, r Burnley, r Bury street

*Stansfield, Joseph and Sons, Little Hul

Taylor, Samuel, Garside street, r West bank, Chorley new road

Taylor, Thomas, Lever street, r Park hill place

Thomason & Son, Mill hill, r High bank

Thompson, John, Farnworth

Topp and Hindley, Farnworth

Walker, Robert, Chorley street, r Kensington place

Whowell, Alexander, Salt Pie yard, Deansgate, r High street

Wild, John, Salt Pie yard, Deansgate, r Spring gardens

Cotton Waste Dealers.

Brearley and Parkinson, Exchange street, r Atherton, r Spring gardens

Briercliffe, Thomas, Old hall street, r 193 Folds road

Collings. William, Folds street, r Higher Bridge street

Devenport, John, Old hall street r Hulme street

Dearden, Oliver, Grime street, r Mawdsley street

Haslam, James, Folds street, r 13 Bath street

Haslam, John. Princess street

Holden, Robert, Old hall street, r Knowsley street

Knott, Daniel, Mealhouse lane, r Newport street

Parkinson, James, Howell croft

Wild, Joseph, Blackhorse street

Cotton Yarn Dealers.

Balshaw, Thomas, 11 Bridge street

Wardle, James, 115 Bark street|

Curriers & Leather Dealers.

Ainsworth, Richard, 24, Bridge street

Ainsworth, George, Deansgate, r Kay st.

Bates, John, Ashburner street

Crosland, Joseph, (and dealer in Gutta Percha) Mawdsley street, r High view (See advertisement.)

Haslam, Robert and P. Deansgate

Lawson, Robert, Bank street

Lomax, Philip, Howell croft

Ormrod, Thomas, Taylor brow, r St George's terrace

Pilkington, John, Knowsley street, r Higher Bridge street

Walker, William and Charles, Ridgway gates, r Newport terrace, r Green hill

Wallwork, Joseph, Chapel street, L.B. r Chorley road

Dentists.

Aspinall, Joseph, Deansgate, r Wood st.

Patrick, Robert, 2 Wood street *(See Advertisement)*

Distiller.

Hall, Rowland, *Bolton Distillery,* Nelson square

Draftsmen,

Dixon, Thomas, Derby street

France, Frank, Castlehill

Haworth, Richard, 7 Chorley road

Lawrie, William, Bath street

Salter, Robert, Bath street

Temperley, John Pugh, Bradford place

Thomson, James, 67 higher Bridge st.

Thornley, J. Derby street

Dyers.

Bradshaw Works Company; John Cross, resident partner, Bradshaw hall

Chadwick, John, and Brother,Eagley

Cunliffe, Samuel, Churchgate

Darbyshire, Smith, & Taylor, Egerton Dye Works

Daniels, H. Bridgman street

Diggle, Abraham, Tonge

Flinn, William, 172 Folds road

Grandin, Francis, Turton street

Hardcastle, James, and Co., Firwood & Bradshaw

Horrocks, Samuel, Kersley

Mather, Thomas, Farnworth

Shaw, Allan, back Oswald street

Taylor, Joseph, Taylor brow

Watson, R. Kay street

Wright, John, sen. Deansgate

Wright, John, jun. Nelson square

Earthenware Dealers.

(See also Glass and China Dealers.)

Haywood, Alice & Esther, Turton street

Hurst, Thomas, 36 Old Hall street

Jackson, Samuel, Newport street

Mitchell, Charles, 34 Old Hall street

Mitchell, James, 35 ditto

Platt, Thomas, Brinks brow

Tatlock, James, 29 Old Hall street

Turner, Alice, Folds road

Walker, Mary Ann, Lever street

Woodhead, Mary, Cross street

Eating-house Keepers.

Airey, Richard, Hotel street

Aspinall, Thomas, Bradshawgate

Barket, Abraham, Market place

Greenhalgh, Robert, Manor street
Hamer, Samuel, Mealhouse-lane
Knight, Margaret, Churchgate
Nelson, James, Deansgate
Sharples, James, Churchgate
Tonge, Thomas, Bradshawgate

Engineers and Millwrights.

Dean, A. and Co., *Phœnix Foundry; r* Mrs. Alice Dean and Mr. A. Dean, Goodwin House, Folds road
Dobson & Metcalf, Kay street; *r* Back o'th' bank; West bank, Chorley new rd.
Hardman, John, (the Exors.) *Coronation Foundry,* Gas street; *r* Chorley road
Hick, Benj. & Son, *Soho Works; r* Highfield
Jackson & Bro: *Wharf Foundry; r* Mr. **J. H.,** Chorley new road; Mr. T. C., Bradford terrace, Haulgh
Knight & Wood, *Victoria Foundry,* Garside street; *r* Spring cottage; Chorley new road
Musgrave, John, Son & Heaton, *Globe Iron Works,* Kay street; *r* 59 Higher Bridge st.; Albert place; St George's terrace
Rothwell & Co. *Union Foundry,* Black horse street; *r* Sunning hill
Thompson & Cole, *Hope Foundry,* St George's street

Engravers.

Kay, Henry, *(Copper-plate & Lithographic Printer)* 145, higher Bridge st.—*See Advertisement.*
Mancor, James, Bridge street
Mc'Donnal, Michael, Howel croft

Farmers

Baron, William, Cockey moor
Beddows, Richard, Halliwell road
Booth, Luke, Little Bolton hall
Brindle, John, Horrocks fold
Hibbert, John, Willows
Longworth, William, Horrocks fold
Mayoh, Miles, Higher End, Astley bridge
Ormrod, Thomas, Cannon street
Scholfield, Richard, Blackburn str. L. B.
Heaton and Brimelow, Derby street
Towler, John, Higher end
Tunstall, Edmund, Pike's lane
Young, John, High street

File Manufacturers.

R. J. & C. Chadbond, Moor lane

Fire and Life Offices.

See Almanack cover.

Flax Dressers.

Jackson, Michael, Smith street
Settle, John, Crown street

Fruiterers.

Ball, John, Bradshawgate
Calderbank, Richd., 12 New Marketplace
Reynolds, Maxwell, Bradshawgate
Salt, Thomas, Bradshawgate

Furniture Brokers.

Brierley, Ann, Bradshawgate
Brierley, Henry, Exchange street
Brierley, Thomas, Newport street
Bromley, William, Great Moor street
Butler, William, Hulme street L.B.
Frost, Joshua, Deansgate
Graham, Thomas, Bridge street
Harpe, John, Farnworth
Hawthorn, Henry, Great Moor street
Knowles, Peter, Moor lane

Milligan, Wm. Newport st—See Advert.
Moor, James, Great Moor street
Parkinson, James, Cheapside
Sanderson, William, Great Moor street
Slater, Thomas, Cheapside
Taylor, Edward, New Market place
Winder, James, Old hall street
Worsley, James, Old hall street

Ginger Beer Makers.

Cartwright, Wright, Hotel street
Harwood, John, Cheapside
Walmsley, Thomas, (Soda water, Ale, & Porter dealer) Nelson square, *r* Clarence street
Wolfenden, Joseph, Bridgman street

Glass and China Dealers.

(See also Earthenware Dealers)
Armstrong, Samuel, New Market place
Field, John, Crown street
Lee, Richard, Cheapside
Nicholls, Charles, Nelson square

Grocers and Tea Dealers.

(See Tea Dealers ; also, Shopkeepers.)
Ackroyd, William, New Market place
Ainsworth, Richard, New Market place
Baxendale, Thomas, Deansgate
Baxendale, William Deansgate
Bullivant, J. O., Bridge street
Challinor, John, Deansgate
Challinor, Ralph, Deansgate
Challinor, John, Moor lane
Crompton, John, Farnworth
Crook, John, Manor street
Crook, Robert, (wholesale) Cheapside, *r* No. 21 Mawdsley street
Crook, Robert, Farnworth
Dauber, Thomas, Deansgate
Duffy, Henry and Co., Farnworth
Eaton, Thomas and Co 1 Market place
Fawell, George, Mill street & Cheapside
Fielding, Charlotte, Bradshawgate
Fitznewton, James, 32 Deansgate
Healy, Jeremiah, Deansgate
Hesketh, Thomas, (wholesale) Bank str. *r* Summer field
Hoyle, John, Blackburn street, L.B.
Jackson, John, Newport street
Kay, George, Bradshawgate
Lever, James, Manor street, *r* Wood str.
Lomax, John, Barn street, L.B.
Lomax, William, Halliwell
Mason, George, Deansgate
Mason, William, Bank street
Maude, Isaac, Derby street
Mayoh, John, Bradshawgate
Mayor, Richard, Wholesale, Old hall street; retail, Oxford street
Morris, James, 141 and 152 Deansgate, *r* Chorley new road
Morris, David, 17 Mill street, L.B.
Moscrop, Thos. Barn street & Folds road
Orrel, J. B. Manor street
Porrit, William, Bradshawgate
Salt, George, 6 Deansgate
Salt, Ellnor, Churchgate
Scholes, Benjamin, Little Lever
Smalley, Robert, Bradshawgate
Smith, James, Manor street
Steele, J. J. Churchgate
Stockdale, Joseph C., Bank street
Stones, William, Market street
Tatton, Joseph, Ashburner street, corner of Old hall street

Threlfal, Thomas and Co. New Market
Topping, R. C. Deansgate
Turner, Joseph, Oxford street
Warbutton, William, 12 Deansgate
Whittle, L. Low, Market street
Withnel, E. Kay street, L.B.
Wood, Henry, Cheapside

Haberdashers.

Collier, Joseph, Farnworth
Cooke, John Pratt, Churchgate
Daniels, Matthew, Cheapside
Diggle, Thomas, Bradshawgate
Haddock, Samuel, (& Dyer) Bank street
Hassal, Ann, 197 Folds road
Heaton, John, Folds road
Heywood, James. Hulme street
Hilton, John, Hulme street
Hughes, Daniel, Oxford street
Mc Hale Luke, Cheapside
Morris, William, Kay street
Nurse, George, New Market place
Ross. Robert, Bradshawgate
Smith, James, Manor street
Stockdale, Mary, Farnworth
Taylor, Richard, 160 Folds road

Hair Dressers.

Berrey, James, 4 Manor street
Bragg, John, (& Agent) Deansgate
Briscoe, M., Bradshawgate
Calvert, George, Churchgate
Chambers, Thomas, Moor lane
Crossland, Robert, Churchgate
Dobson, John, Shaw street
Fallows, John, Bradshawgate
Heald, James, Great Moor street
Hipplewell, Robert, Deansgate
Houlston, John Deansgate
Howson, John, Deansgate
Isherwood, John, Bradshawgate
Mc Grath, Terrence, Manor street
Monks, James, Moor lane
Morris, Thomas, Deansgate
Orrell, William, Exchange street West
Parkinson, George, 5, Bridge street
Parkinson. William, Folds road
Redford, John, Folds road
Redford, William, Newport street
Sager, Thomas, Howell croft
Shaw, William, Bradshawgate
Staton, Samuel, Bradshawgate
Thornley, William, Manor street
Turnbull, James, New Market place
Wilding, Edward, Derby street
Wright, John, Crown street
Yates, William, Deansgate

Hardware Dealers.

Collins, James, Turton street
Coop, Wm., Newport street & Cheapside
Haworth, John, Derby street
Moore, Edward, Exchange street West

Hatters.

Cheetham, Samuel, 33 Deansgate
Fletcher, Abraham Bradshawgate
Hanesworth, T. Deansgate
London Hat Company, Deansgate
Morley, John, Deansgate
Morley, Robert, Deansgate

Hay and Straw Dealers.

Greenhalgh, Henry. Mawdsley street
Thornton, Joseph, Old hall street

Heald Knitters.

Mitchell, John, Falcon street
Taylor, Abraham, Ainsworth

Hosiers.

Cooke, John Pratt, Churchgate
Hughes, Daniel. Oxford street
Latham, John, 8 Deansgate
Mc Hale, Luke, Cheapside
Nurse, George, 6, New Market place

Iron and Brass Founders.

(For residences, &c.. *see also Brass Founders & Machine Makers*)
Albinson, John, junr. Deansgate
Dean, A. & Co., Folds road
Dobson and Metcalfe, Kay street
Hardman, John, the Exors. Gas street
Hick, Benjamin, and Son, Soho works
Jackson and Brothers. Wharf Foundry
Knight and Wood, Garside street
Lord, James. & Co., Foundry street, *r* Bridgman street, *r* Sydney street
Musgrave, Son, & Heaton, Kay street
Peat, Robert, Farnworth
Rigby, Ed., Queen st, *r* Bradshawgate
Rothwell. & Co., Union Foundry, Black horse street
Thompson & Cole, St. George's street

Iron Founders.

(*See also preceding list*)
Almond, Walker, Farnworth
Hodkinson & Marsden Folds road, *r* Waterloo street, *r* Back Mill street
Kirkman, Jas. Howell croft, *r* Wood st.
Roscow, James, Farnworth
Threlfall, Richard, Bridgman place
Yardley, William, Moses gate

Iron Masters.

Rushton and Eckersley, Moor lane, *r* West bank. Chorley new road; *r* do.

Ironmongers.

Colman, Mary, Bank street
Higson, P. Deansgate. (opp. Mrkt. st.)
Higson, William, 144 Deansgate
Thwaites, Thomas, Deansgate
Walmsley, Thomas, Oxford street
Wolstenholme, Samuel, Oxford street

Joiners.

See Timber Merchants.
Adamson, Richard, Derby street
Banks, John, Crook street
Barber, Solomon, Lever street
Barlow, John, Dawes' street
Blackley, Thomas, Bow street
Bleakley, Thomas, Princess street
Chambers, William, Bourne street
Charnley, Richard, All Saints' street
Chorlton, John, Kersley
Collins, James, Falcon street
Cooper, Francis, Weston street
Crackstone, T. Great Moor street
Dobie, William, Little Lever
Gibson, Thomas, Wood street
Graham, Thomas, Bridge street
Greenhalgh, William, Mawdsley street
Gregory, William, Shuttle street
Hamer, Robert, Bourne street
Heywood, Peter, Little Lever
Holt, John, Sharples
Holden, J. Hulme street
Isherwood, Wm. Middle street
Kirkman, Robert, Dawes' street
Moleyneux, Ed. Newport street
Nicholson, Oliver, Blackburn street
Nicholson, Joseph, Great Moor street
Parkinson, James, Commission street
Scott, Moses, (and Undertaker) Kay st.

50

Smith, Moses, (*Undertaker*) 10 Turton st.
Stone, Wm. Blackburn street L.B.
Taylor, Joseph, St George's road
Welsby, John, Farnworth
Westby, Jonathan, Derby street

Land Agents and Surveyors.

Corn, Edward, 7 Newport street
Cross, Giles, Market street, *r* Higher bridge street
Hall, Phineas, (road) Falcon street
Horrocks, James, Nelson square
Jackson Joseph, 169 Bridge street, *r* Castle hill
Kearsley, John, Folds street
Lever, Thomas, Church wharf—See Adv
Lomax, James, Mealhouse lane, *r* Barn street, L.B.
Nicholson, William, Ridgway gates
Piggot, George, Bradshawgate, *r* there and Hardman fold, Great Lever

---

Law Stationers.

Owen, Thomas, Exchange street east, *r* Hotel street
Tyrrel, Thomas, Chancery lane
Wharton, G. F. Acres' field

Linen & Woollen Drapers.

Cottrill, John, Market street (see advertisement
Hebden, Jonathan, Deansgate, (corner of Bridge street)
Henry and Co, Deansgate, (corner of Market street) *r* Park hill—See Advert.
Martin and Co. Deansgate
Orton, John, 148, Deansgate
Shaw, William, 1 Market place
Skelton, Peter, Cheapside
Skelton, Charles, Cheapside
Steadman, William, Farnworth
Stockdale, Richard, Deansgate, 'corner of Bank street

Linen Drapers.

Bateson, Henry, Deansgate, corner of Bradshawgate
Bradley, John, 107 Turton street, L.B.
Crompton, Robert, Little Lever
France, Jessie, Blackburn street, L.B.
Highton, John, 172 Bridge street
Holden, John, Derby street
Horrocks, John, Jun., Deansgate
Horrocks, Lawrence, Market street
Hulme, C. 1 Deansgate
Latham, John, Deansgate
Lomax, Mary, Farnworth
Moscrop, Robert, Deansgate
Moscrop, J. (wholesale) Cross Axe Entry, Deansgate, *r* higher Bridge street
Moxon, Nathaniel, 1 Market street
Openshaw, John, Blackburn street
Scholes, Thomas, Farnworth
Schofield, John, 10 Kay street, L.B.
Tait, James M., Market st. (See advert.

Linen Drapers & Tea Dealers— Travelling.

Bell, James, 97 Bark street
Clapperton, Robert, Wood street
Dixon, Robert, 94 Bark street
Hannay, William, Wood street
Hill, Edward, 100 Bark street
Holliday, Wm. 24 Bridge street
Isherwood, Joseph, 6 High street, L.B.
Lockhart, John, 97 Bark street
Mc'Connel, John, 93 Bark street

Mc'Kinnel, Andrew, Wood street
Platt, Thomas, 60 Brinks brow
Shaw, John, 94 Bark street
Watson, John, Silverwell street
Watson, Wm. Bark street
Young, Sarah, 90 Bark street

Machine Makers.

(See *Engineers, Iron & Brass Founders*.)
Albinson, John, Deansgate
Dean, A. & Co. Folds road
Dobson & Metcalf, Kay street
Jackson & Bro: Wharf Foundry
Lord, James, & Co. Foundry street
Peat, Robert, Farnworth
Rigby, Edward, Queen street
Ryder, William, Bark street
Threlfall, Wm. Bridgman street
Yardley, William, Farnworth

Managers and Foremen.

Arrowsmith, Thomas, Victoria terrace
Banks, John, Hanover street
Bell, George, Bridgman street
Birchall, James, do.
Bispham, George, 153 do.
Bland, E. Bath street
Bowker, Abraham, Deansgate
Broughton, Jos. do.
Craigh, J. Bridgman street
Davies, Thomas, Green street
Dean, James, 22 Foundry street
Dootson, Richard, Lime street
Draper, Joseph, 170 Folds road
Edwards, George, Tipping street
Greenhalgh, James, Crook street
Halsby, E. 59 higher Bridge street
Hamer, Peter, Haigh street
Hamer, Wm. Lever street
Hargreaves, Henry, Mill hill
Hemnings, 61 higher Bridge street
Higson, Jas. Bridgman place
Hill, Wm. Farnworth
Homer, Jas. 69 Crook street
Howard, John, 1 Foundry street
Hozdack, Geor. Folds road
Hughes, Joseph Chas. 63 high. Bridge st
Johnson, John, Farnworth
Kaywood, Peter, Newport street
Leonard, Jas. Lever street
Longworth, Henry, Mill hill place
Ludlane, John, Kay street
Mc'Cann, John, Bridgman street
Mitchell, Reuben, Derby street
Musgrave, Jonath. higher Bridge street
Musgrave, John do.
Musgrave, James, do.
Ormston, Wm. Derby street
Orrell, J. Derby street
Owen, Robt. Smith street
Patterson, Thos. Farnworth
Peacock, George, Commission street
Price, T. L. Blackburn street
Reeves, Jas. Brinks brow
Ridings, A. 71 higher Bridge street
Riley, Jas. Middle street
Seddon, Jas. 2 Waterloo street
Sherratt, Robt. 32 York street
Smith, George, Darcy Lever
Swift, Chas. Bridgman street
Talbott, Thos. 15 Sydney street
Taylor, Robt. Lever street
Thistlethwaite, C. B. Folds road
Thompson, R. Bridge street
Tillotson, Jno. Bank cottage L.B.

Toulmin, George, Falcon street
Walker, Jas. Joiners' square
Waterhouse, John, Bridgman street
Whittaker, Jas. Vernon bank
Wilkinson, Jas. Ward street
Wilson, Jas. Smith street
Wood, Jas. Folds road

Malt and Hop Dealers.
Binks, George, Mealhouse lane
Sawdon, Thomas & Co. Bridge street

Manuf. of Counterpanes.
Baron, John, Bradshawgate
Bateman, Phil. & Thos. Lever st. *r* Salford
Bond, John, Union buildings
Bury, Ellis, Lever street
Crook, Peter and Son, St George's place
Hadfield, Richard, Moor lane
Hampson, Rd. Bridgman street
Haslam, Jas. & Sons, Black horse st. *r* Chorley old road
Haslam, Roger, High street. [Park hill
Haslam, Roger, Black horse street; *r*
Haslam, Wm. Lum street
Haslam, John, Mill street
Hodkinson, G. Bridgman st. *r* Manchtr
Holme, Richd. Commission st. *r* Manchr
Hutchinson, John & Wm. Goodwin st.
Lever. Thos. Kay street
Lever, Henry, Johnson st. *r* Newport st.
Lomax, Jacob & Son, Goodwin street; *r* Westhoughton; Folds road
Longworth, Joseph, Bridgman street
Mitchell, John, Dale street; *r* Water st.
Myerscough, Steele and Co. Bullock st. *r* Silverwell street
Nightingale, Rd. Lum st. *r* St Geo.'s pl.
Openshaw, Jas. Darcy Lever
Orrell, Thos. Grime st. *r* Chorley road
Pearson T. & Son, Bradshaw st. *r* do
Phethean, Josph. Haulgh [Manchester
Pownall & Lomax, Old acres; *r* Bowden
Taylor, J. Haulgh. [65 higher Bridge st
Vickers, J. Independent st. *r* Tipping st

Manuf. of Dimities & Quiltings
Barlow, Jas. Green street; *r* Folds road
Blair & Burton, Foundry st; *r* Mill hill house; Green bank house
Heywood John & Son, High street
Johnson, Jabez, back Bridgman street; *r*
Swan, Saml. Rose hill [Manchester
Taylor, T. Chancery lane; *r* Welling. place

Manuf. of Muslins.
Barnes, Thos. Barn street; *r* Tipping place
Bayley James & John, Shambles; *r* Newport place; Newport terrace
Birch, Thos. Market street; *r* High street
Brodie Hugh & Son, Moor lane; *r* Vic: terrace
Cannon, Wm. Chancery lane; *r* Park hill
Clayton, Alexr. Back 'oth' bank
Cocksey, Thos. Chorley new road
Cooke, W. W. & Jas. Bridge st; *r* Kensington place; St George's street
Crook Peter and Son, St George's place
Cunliffe, George, lower Bridgman street
Cunliffe, Richd. Byng street
Davenport, Edward, Lever street
Eckersley, Robt. Flackburn street
Finney, Jas. Lever street
Green, John, Manchester road
Harwood, Peter, Falcon street
Haslam Jas and Son, Black horse street
Haslam, J. & Co. St Geo. ges st *r* Mr J. Chorley road; Messrs. R. and A., Lark hill
Haslam, Roger, Flack house street
Hitchen, Jona. Ashbnrner st. *r* Park hill
Howarth, Geo. Derby street
Knight, Henry, Churchgate
Lomax Abraham, Folds road
Mallett, Jno. Mawdsley st. *r* St Geo.'s st.
Mather, Jas. Falcon street
Mitchell, John, Barn street
Ormrod & Hardcastle, Flash street
Nuttall, Zachias, Harwood
Nuttall, Saml. Shambles; *r* Commer. Inn
Parkinson, Rd. Blackburn street G. B.
Rostron, Thos. Bridgman street
Seed and Seddon, Breightmet
Sharples, Arthur, Independent street
Tootal Edward & Co. Stanley street
Webster, Martha, Blackburn street
Welsby, Thos. do.
Wolfenden, Jno. Pikes lane

Medicine Venders & Herbalists
Banks, J. Folds road
Clark, Richd. Spring gardens
Flitcroft, Ellis, Sydney street
Oldham, Peter, Newport street
Roberts, Wm. Deansgate
Shaw and Grimshaw, Bridgman street

Medical Galvanists.
Chamberlain, W. H. Newport st; See Advertisement.
Flitcroft. Ellis, Sydney st. [

Dress Makers.

Ashworth, Ellen, Green street
Atkinson, Sarah, Old acres
Ballis, Mary, Bradshawgate
Baron, Sarah, 140 Derby street
Barrett, Betsy, 177 Folds road
Baxter, William, Cheapside
Birchby, A. Old acres
Bennet, Jane, Barn street
Bradshaw, Mary, Chorley st. l. b.
Bond Ellen, Silverwell street
Booth, Jane, Bullock street, l. b.
Brockleband, Betsy, Kay st. l. b.
Brown, Hannah, Great moor st.
Buckley, M. Lever street
Chadwick, A. Gas street
Chorley, Betty, 68 Howel croft
Cochrane, H. Spring gardens
Coe, M. 49 Howel croft
Coop, Mary, Churchgate
Cradock, Elizabeth, Deansgate
Crompton, Mary, 171 Bridge st.
Crompton, Helen, Bradshawgate
Crompton, Margaret, Farnworth
Cross, Ellen, Farnworth
Coulston Martha, Newport street

Daniels, Matthew, Cheapside
Davy, L. Newport street
Dixon, Sarah, York street
Dixon, Hannah, 160 Bridge street
Drinkwater, E. Moor lane
Driver, Catherine, Folds road
Eckersley, Alice, Derby street
Edge, M. 85 Black horse street
Edge, Ann, Blackburn street
Ellison, A. Bridgeman street
Fairclough, Mary, Water street
Fiddler, Mary Ann, Fold street
Fogg, E. Great moor street
Foxon, Elizabeth, Spring gardens
Graham, Elizabeth, 78 Kay street
Greenhalgh, Mary, Kay street
Greenhalgh, Margaret, Folds road
Green, Jane, Brown street
Grime, Esther, Deansgate
Haigh, Catherine. Bury street
Hamer, E. Bullock street
Harrison, Betsy, Bridgman place
Hawksworth, Esther, Bullock st.
Harrison, C. 3 Black horse street
Heywood, Betsy Turton street

Henry, Harriet, Hulme street
Hilton, B; 90 Bridge street
Holden, Ann, Derby street
Hood, Sarah, Bullock street
Houghton, E. 20 Howel croft
Hyder, M. A. Hulme street
Johnson, Ann, Halliwell road bar
Kay, Alice, Kay street
Kay, Margaret, Chorley street
Kellet. Ellen, Deansgate
Kirkham, Maria, Weston street
Knott, Hannah, Green street
Laurie, Grace, Bath street
Lawton, Mary, Weston street
Lee,, Jane, back Coe street
Leftwich, A. howel croft
Leslie, Mary, Union street
Lumley, Jane, Bridgman street
Marsden, Jane, 162-3 Bridge st.
Marsden, Amelia, Weston street
Marsden, Eliza, Green street
Marsden, E. 77 Blackhorse street
Middleton, L. Charles street
Mort. Sarah, Farnworth
Nightingale, Mary, Newport st.

Noble, Sarah, higher Bridge street
Ormston, *Mary Ann*, Derby street
Orrel, A. 30 Ashburner street
Parr, *Jane*, Bridgemau place
Partington, Elizabeth, Weston st
Pennington, Betsy, 107 Kay st.
Pickering, Alice, Coe at
Pilling, R. Crook place
Pollit, Mary, Bullock street
Rimmington, *Elizabeth*, 4 High st.
Rose, Margaret, Mawdsley street
Ritson, J. Hanover street

Rothwell, Mary Ann, 5 High st.
Seddon, *A.* Cross street
Seymour, Betsy Deansgate
Schofield, Eliza, Independent st.
Sharples, Sarah J. Newport st.
Sharples, Ann, Lupton street
Shawcross, M. Lupton street
Smith, Mary, Duncan street
Speed, Elizabeth, Deansgate
Standring, M. Moor lane
Swarbrick, Elizh. Bradshawgate
Swift, Catherine, 111 Derby st.

Swift, Mary, Garside street
Thornley, B. Fletcher street
Tong, Alice, Bradshawgate
Tudor, Mary & Ellen, Bradfd. sqr.
Walkden, Jane, Great moor street
Walker Jane, 69 Blackhorse st.
Walls, Ellen, Blakebro' buildings
Ward, Esther, Queen street
Ward, Amelia, Turton street
Whalley, N. W. 34 Newport st.
Winder, M. 38 higher Bridge st.
Yates, Ellen, 18 Weston street

Millwrights.

See Engineers and Millwrights.

Music & Instrument Sellers.

Hardman, Thomas, Market square
Fawcett, John, Sen. Bridge street
Jackson, Richard, Crown street
Parvin, William, Bradshawgate

Newspapers and Periodicals.

Bolton Advertiser :—A. Mackie, 95 Bark street, Publisher; (on the first of every month). *See Advertisement.*
Bolton Almanac :—Henry Bradbury, Deansgate, Publisher; (yearly).
Bolton Chronicle : — William Bridge, Publisher; Jas. Hudsmith, Manager; Stephen Rothwell, 80 Folds road, Reporter. Every Saturday Morning. (The Chronicle is the only Newspaper in Bolton at present, and is larger and better got up than most country papers)
Bolton Temperance Messenger : William Smith, Market st. AdvertisementAgent.

Organ Builders.

Jackson, R. Crown street *(See Advertis.)*
Parvin, William, Bradshawgate

Overlookers.

Collins, James, Salt pie yard,
Darbyshire, *John*, back Spring gardens
Dewsnap, George, Spaw lane
Fishwick, William, Queen street
Greenhalgh, William, Bradshawgate
Greenhalgh, John, Woods court
Halliwell, Robert, higher Bridge street
Heywood, James, 3 Mill hill place
Hiton, John, Bridge street
Horrocks, William, Derby street
Jones, Thomas, Lever street
Kay, John, Halliwell
Kennerdale, John, Howell croft
Makinson, William, higher Bridge street
Mort, Peter, Smith street
Nicholson, Thomas, Newport street
Nicholson, William, Mill hill terrace
Osbeldestone, James, Barn street
Rawsthorn, —, Cross street
Redford, Benjamin, Brinks brow
Rigby, James, Barracks brow
Slater, William, Kay street
Williams, William, Bow street

Painters and Paper Hangers.

*Those marked thus * are Plasterers also.*
*Booth, John & Thomas, Bullock street
*Booth, Richard, Kay street
*Booth, Luke, Turton street
Caton, John, V. Howell croft
*Chippendale, John, back Acres' field
Coop, Robert, Church wharf
Daggett, S. Crown st.; *r* higher Bridge st.
Dyson, Aaron, 10 Princess street
Fogg, John, Water street, (Paper hanger)
Greenhalgh and Peat, Silverwell court, Bradshawgate; *r* 14 Great Moor street; *r* High bank, Haulgh

Hilton, *Wm.*, Hulme st. (Paper hanger)
*Holden, Richard, junr., 42 Deansgate—
*Holden, Rich., Nelson sqr. [*See Adver.*
*Horrobin, Thomas, Well street
Knowles, James, Blackhorse street
Leach, *Thomas*, Mealhouse lane
Leach, Robert, Hotel street
Lee, Squire, Old Acres
Lord, David, Kearsley
Mitchell, Thomas, Grundy fold
Morris, David, Well street
Morris, William, Derby street
Moss, Thomas, Barn street
Pilling, *James*, Sharples
Pilkington, William, Taylor brow; *r* 194 Folds road—*See Advertisement.*
*Platt, John, Old hall street
Rothwell, Edward, Folds street, Shop and *r* Bradshawgate
*Speakman, John, Mill street
*Stewart, Michael, Spring gardens
Tong, William, Bradshawgate
Tong, James, St. George's street

PaperMakers.

Crompton, J. & T. B. Farnworth; *r* Mr. T. B. Farnworth; *r* Mr. Fletcher, Prestolee; Mr. Ed. Barlow, Prestolee
Crompton, Roger, Kearsley
Crook, Thomas, & Son, Hall i'th' Wood
Knowles and Crook, Eagley Mill
Mangnall, W. & W. Springfield Haulgh
Turner, Charles, Higher Sharples

Paper Merchants.

Hughes, Robert, 5 Exchange street East *r* Oxford street.—*See Advertisement.*
Nelson, Geo. Bow st., *r* St George's ter.

Pawnbrokers.

Bradshaw, Mary Ann, Deansgate and Hotel street
Duckworth, John, Exchange street Wst.
Greenhalgh, William, Rothwell's court, Black horse street
Hamer, John, back Turton street
Holden, William, 173 Kay street
Horrocks, William, Ashburner street
Horrocks, John, Weston street
Horrocks, John Barn street
Merginson, Robert, Crook street
Markland, Alice, Blackburn street
Norman, D. Bradshawgate *r Blackburn*
Nuttal, Ann, Deansgate
Orrel, Alice, Kay street
Powell, Thomas, 184 Folds road
Smith, Robert, 51 Blackburn street
Wiggins, Charles, 12 New Market place
Whittle. Hezekiah, Deansgate
Wilson, Nathaniel, Manor street
Yates, John, Cheapside ; *r* Park hill

Physicians.

Anderton, G. L. Farnworth
Black, J. Haulgh
Chadwick, S. T. Manchester road
Haworth, Thomas, Wood street

53

Picker Makers.
For Power and Hand Looms.
Blakeborough, John, (Picking bands, Hide & Sizing Dealer,) Coe street
Bromley, James, Derby street
Dixon, Richard, do.

Plumbers and Glaziers.
Allsebrook, Wm. Taylor brow
Bancroft, Wm. Sharples
Burrow, Jno. Brown street
Clifford, Roger, Crown street
Fletcher, Charles, Moorlane
Green, John, Brinks brow
Grime, Jas. Blackburn street, L.B.
Grimshaw, Wm. Lever street L.B.
Harwood, Richd. Charles street
Haworth, James, Moor lane
Howard, James, Bradshawgate
Makinson, Hugh, Knowsley street
Markland, Wm, Newport street
Nelson, Samuel, Bridge street
Nuttall, John, Farnworth
Phethean, Wm. Chancery lane
Richardson, James, Crook street
Rothwell, Peter, 143 Kay street
Roscow, Robt. Farnworth
Shaw, John, Halliwell
Travers, John, Churchgate
Travers, Henry, Bradshawgate
Welch, Ellis, Crook street
Wood, Jno. Chorley street

Printers—Letter-Press.
(See also Booksellers and Printers.)
Bridge, William, Chronicle office
Burrel, John, Crown street
Cook, Joseph, Farnworth
Kenyon, R. Oxford street; r 13 School st.
Morris, Thomas, Oxford st. r Well street
Roberts, Thomas, Bradshawgate
Staton, James, Exchange street

Professors and Teachers.
Fawcett, Jno. sen. (Music) Bridge street
Fawcett, Jno. junr. do. do.
Hardman, Thomas, do. New Mrkt.sq.
Mackie, Alexr. (Short Hand Writing.—See Advertisement) 95 Bark street
Rothwell, Selim, (Drawing) Bradshawgt.
Winder, D. (Drawing) higher Bridge st

Provision Dealers.
(See also Shopkeepers.)
Bateson, B. Kay street
Broughton, Wm. Blackburn street
Dickson & Co. Deansgate
Eastham, Matthew, 54 Kay street
Eckersley, Robt. Hotel street
Garrett, Alexr. Kay street
Gerrard, Joseph, Blackburn street
Grundy, Edmund, Crook street
Hedley, Robt. 10 Weston street
Horan, M. Oxford street
Lever, Thos. Mill street
McCormick, P. Deansgate
McCormick, F. 67 Deansgate
Openshaw, Jno. Blackburn street
Openshaw, Wm. Farnworth
Scoweroft, Thos. Bradshawgate
Stout, Edwd. Market street
Steadman, Jno 6 Bridge street
Steele, J. J. (Union Shop) Bradshawgate
Winterburn, Jno. Kersley
Wallwork, Jno. Farnworth
Wiseman, Wm. Crown street
Wiseman, Wm. Deansgate

Quarry Owners.
Ainsworth, Peter, Smithills hall—Roger Walsh, Agent
Hampson, Ann, Little Hulton
Walsh, Jas. Moor lane

Rag Dealers.
Conlin, John, Newport street
Holden, Robt. Old Hall st. r Knowsley st.
Jump, Mary, 177 Kay street
Leach, Robt. Churchgate
Morris, Wm. Great Moor street
Nelson, Geor. Bow street
Nuttall, Jno. junr. Moor lane; r King st.
Nuttall, Jno. senr. King street
Taylor, Jas. Dawes' street
Welsh, Thos. Folds road and Newport st

Reed Makers.
Dawson, Wm Deansgate
Dewhurst, Jno. Old acres; r Mawdsley st
Greenhalgh, Jno. Bullock street
Grundy, Philip, Cross street
Monks, Jno. Ashburner street
Monks, R. Hulme street
Morris, Jno. Howell croft.

Register Office for Servants.
Fitton, J. All Saints' street
Mather, John, 59 Brinks brow
Platt, Thomas ditto
Santley, Joseph, Mealhouse lane
Swarbrick, E. Bradshawgate

Roller Makers.
Albinson, John, Deansgate
Dobson and Metcalf, Kay street
Rigby, Edward, Queen street
Ryder, Wm. Bark street

Rope and Twine Makers.
Charnock, John, Fletcher street
Kellet, Ellen and Sons, Deansgate
Lloyd, Sarah, 25 Brown street
Lloyd, John, Independent street, L.B
Loftos, James, Old acres
Loftos, Thomas, Bank street; warehouse, Barn street
Platt, William, Bridgman street
Ramsden, Joseph, Cocker lane, L.B. r Latham place
Shepherd, John, Blackburn street
Taylor, Thomas, Derby street
Taylor, George, Union buildings

Saddlers & Harness Makers.
Bolton, John, Blackhorse street
Brown, Thomas, Kersley
Jones, Richard, 48 Bow street
Kay, Thomas, 3 Brown street
Kay, Thomas, Jun. Manor street
Knowles, Thomas, 40 Deansgate
Pendlebury, John, Market street, r Ridgway gates
Rothwell, James, High street, L.B.
Scott, Jacob, Folds road
Smith, Charles, Crown street
Tate, J. Oxford street, r Brinks brow (see advertisement.)

Sharebrokers.
Gorton, James, Bowker's row r lower Bridgman street
Wolfenden, J. R., Silverwell street,

Shopkeepers.
Allen, Robert, Darcey Lever
Alsop, Joseph, Ainsworth

Ashall, Henry, Churchgate
Aspinall, Eliza, Churchgate
Atkinson, Sarah, Brinks brow
Barlow, Nancy, Blakeboro' buildings
Barnes, R. Defence street
Barnes, George, Turton
Barnes, John, Egerton
Barnes, Richard, Blackburn street
Baron, John, Bradshawgate
Baron, Thomas, Green street, L.B.
Bateson, Benjamin, Kay street
Baxter, Esther, Rumworth
Baxter, Thomas, Blackburn street
Bell, R. 32 Bridge street
Bennet, Matthew, Farnworth
Berry, Edmund, Newport street
Berry, John, Folds road
Berry, Ann, Blackhorse street
Beswick, Thomas, 35, St George's st
Birchby, Robert, Bradshawgate
Boardman, James, Old hall street
Boardman, John, Rumworth
Booth. Richard, Fletcher street
Booth, R. Pitt street
Booth, Rhd. Blakeborough buildings
Bowker, Abraham, Deansgate
Bowen, Edward, Smith street, L.B.
Brabain, John, Velvet walks
Bradley, James, Weston street
Bradshaw, John, Bridgman street
Bradshaw, John, Ashburner street
Bradshaw, Ann, 140, Bridge street
Brandwood, Jane, York street
Bray, Luke, Old acres
Bridge, John, Old acres
Briercliffe, Margaret, Folds road
Brierley, Robert, Dixon green
Brimelow, Alice, Kay street
Brockbank, Miles, Kay street
Brockbank, Andrew, 19 Manor street
Bromley, James, Commission street
Bromley, Betty, Bark street
Brooks, James, Darcey lever
Brown, Thomas, Darcey Lever
Bullough, Bullough, 82 Bridge street
Bullough, Richard, Kersley
Burton, Ruth, Pike's lane
Burton, Joshua, Pike's lane
Bury, Jonathon, Folds road
Butterworth, Samuel, Kay street
Carrol, Patrick, Churchgate
Carney, John, Great Moor street
Carribin, James, Newport street
Challinor, Margaret, Mealhouse lane
Challinor, E. Bridgman place
Charlton, J. Blackhorse street
Chorlton, John, Derby street
Clayton, Margaret, 20 Derby street
Cottam, Margaret, Union street
Cousill, Nathan, Dixon green
Crompton, John, Bridgman street
Crompton, Ann, Deansgate
Cronley, John, 109 Turton street
Crossley, John, Turton street
Crook, John, Hulme street, L.B.
Crook, William, 31 Derby street

Crook, John, Derby street
Cumpstey, George, Weston street
Cuerdale, Alice, Folds road
Culshaw, William, Bow street
Cunliffe, James, Manor street
Davenport, James, Stanley street
Dewhurst, John, Water street
Dickinson, Richard, Middle street
Draper, Joseph, Folds road
Drinnan, William, Folds road
Dootson, James, 25 Bridge street
Dootson, H. 67 Blackhorse street
Dootson, Ann, Lum street
Doodson, Thomas, Farnworth
Eastham, Matthew, Kay street
Ellidge, Jane, Green street, L.B.
Fairclough, Robert, Moor lane
Fitton, E. 22 Howell croft
Flanagan, John, Newport street
Fletcher, James, Lever street
Fletcher, Adam, Newport street
Fogg, Thomas, Slater field
Forrest, Henry, John street
Foster, George, Hulme street, L.B.
France, James, 92 Blackburn street
Gerrard, John, 16 Derby street
Gibson, Jane, back Foundry street
Gillet, James, Lever street
Glover, Oliver, Old hall street
Gorse, Alice, Union street
Greenhalgh, Peter, Dawes street
Greenhalgh, Solomon, Middle street
Greenhalgh, Henry, Cockey moor
Greenhalgh, William, Ainsworth
Greenhalgh, R. Howell croft
Gregson, Nicholas, Green street
Grey, David, Blackburn street
Grime, Nancy, Deansgate
Grimshaw, Charles, Lever street, LB
Grundy, Edmund, Crook street
Grundy, Philip, Crook street
Guest, Isaac, Bradshawgate
Hadfield, Richard, Moor lane
Hadfield, William, Derby street
Hadfield, James, Charles street
Haigh, Dorothy, Moor lane
Hall, James, Green street
Hall, Robert, Lever street
Hall, James, Bridge street
Halton, James, Crook street
Hamer, John, Lever street
Hamer, Rachel, Union street
Hamer, John, Hanover street
Hamer, John, back Turton street
Hanna, Robert, Great Moor street
Hampson, Ralph, Deansgate
Hampson, William, Rumworth
Hardiker, James, Blackhorse street
Handley, Bridget, Newport street
Hardman, John, Crook street
Hardman, Elizabeth, Churchgate
Hardy, Isaac, 29 Weston street
Hargreaves, John, White Lion brow
Hargreaves, Richard, Crook street
Harrison, John, Turton street
Hart, William, 84 higher Bridge st.

Haslam, Eliz. Market street, Farnth.
Haslam, Richard, Great moor street
Haslam, Joseph, Old hall street
Haslam, Mary, Fletcher street
Haslam, M. Pitt street
Haywood, Ellen, Brinks bsow
Hesketh, William, higher Bridge str.
Heywood, Mary, King street, Farnh.
Heywood, Ellen, King street, Farnh:
Heywood, Ann, Ashburner street
Hindley, Ann, Market street, Farnth.
Holden, Ann, Deansgate
Holt, William, Moor lane
Holt, John, Middle street
Hood, Thos. Great Moor street
Hopkins, Jos. Manor street
Horrabin, Robert (and tax collector)
  Lever bridge
Horrocks, William, Cockey moor
Horrocks, James, Union street, L.B.
Horrocks, Abraham, Blackburn str.
Howarth, R. Cross street, L.B.
Howarth, Edmund, Shaw street
Howarth, John, Sydney street
Howarth, Edmund, Ainsworth
Howarth, Rich. 92 Commission str.
Jackson, James, Great moor street
Jenyon, Mary, Bridge street
Johnson, James, Bradshawgate
Jones, John, Blackburn street
Jones, Margaret, Deansgate
Kay, Mary, Mill street L.B.
Kay, Thomas, Pike's lane
Kay, Edward, Commission street
Kay, William, Lever street
Kearsley, Sarah, Crook street
Kirkman, John, 9 Back street
Knight, Eliza, Churchgate
Knight, Joseph, Bridge street
Knowles, Thomas, Darcey Lever
Lawrenson, John, Hulme street, L.B
Lawson, Ann, Newport street
Lawson, Robert, Stanley street
Lawton, William, Derby street
Leach, James, Bridgman street
Leigh, Lee, Blackburn street
Lee, James, Bridgman street
Lever, Robt. Kay street, L.B.
Lever, Thomas, Kay street
Lever, Robert, White Lion brow
Lever, Richard, Wharf street
Lever, John, Wharf street
Lindley, Ellis, Market street, Farnth
Lindley, Thos: Nan lane, Farnworth
Loncock, C. Folds road
Longworth, A. Bradshawgate
Lonsdale, John, 78 Kay street
Lumley, James, Bridgman street
Makin, Joseph, Bridgman street
Mc' Garry, Patrick. Ashburner street
Mc' Gill, Andrew, Blackburn street
Malbrough, Geo. North street
Markland, William, Newport street
Marsden, Thomas, Crook street
Marsden, James, Shaw street
Marsh, Richard, Derby street

Meadowcroft, T. 15 Weston street
Mellor, Samuel, Derby street
Middleton , John, Charles street
Miles, Andrew, Market st., Farnwth.
Morris, James, Dawes street
Morris, Margt. Cross street
Morris, James, Kay street
Morris, Robert, Duncan street
Mort, Alice, Deansgate
Nelson, Jane, Hulme street
Newhouse, William, Blackburn rd.
Nicholson, Oliver, Blackburn street
Nicholson, Jos. Great moor street
Nightingale, Jos. Great moor street
Openshaw, Wm. Queen st. Farnwth
Openshaw, A. 17 Weston street
Openshsw, John, Weston street
Orrel, Wm. Cross street
Orrel, Joseph, Union street, L.B.
Owen, Robert, Crook street
Parker, Sarah, Bridgman place
Pasquil, Hen. Rumworth
Pearce, Jno. Union street, L.B.
Pearson, Hen Derby street
Pendlebury, Jas. Halliwell road
Pendlebury, Phœbe, Ashburner str.
Phethean, Joseph, Great moor street
Pilkington, Edward, 61 Bark street
Poole, Hen. Cross street
Prestwich, Rob. Dixon green
Ridings, Joseph, Wharf street
Richardson, Rob. White Lion brow
Richley, Dalton, Charles street
Rigby, Alice, Deansgate
Rigby, John, Deansgate
Rigby, Wm. John street
Rigby, Benj. Falcon street
Riley, Edward, Bridgman street
Robinson, James, Blackhorse street
Ross, Michael, Bradshawgate
Ross, Robt. Bradshawgate
Rothwell, Nath. Cnurchgate
Rothwell, Mary, Fletcher street
Rothwell, J. Lever street, L.B.
Ryley, James, Cannon street
Rylie, Wm. Pike's lane
Scholes, Lydia, Cockey moor
Scholes, Richard, Middle Hulton
Scholfield, Peter, Cross street
Scowcroft, Egbert, Ainsworth
Seddon, Isaac, Deansgate
Seddon, Margt. Chancery lane
Sharp, Thos. King street, Farnwth.
Shaw, Edward, 44 Bow street
Shepherd, Christopher, Lever street
Silcock, Ann, Rumworth
Simcock, James, Newport street
Smith, James, King street
Smith, William, Derby street
Spencer, James, Darcey Lever
Stead, William, Ashburner street
Steer, R. Pitt street
Stones, Wm. 126 Blackburn st. L.B.
Sutcliffe, Wright, Crook street
Suttle, Thos. Lum street

Taylor, James, Darcey Lever
Taylor, John, 157 Folds road
Taylor, Mary, 178 Folds road
Taylor, John, Old acres
Thirlwind, John, Bradshawgate
Thomason, John, Cross street, L.B.
Thornley, Jon. Folds road
Tomlinson, Rich. Shaw street
Tonge, James, Stanley street
Tonge, Jno. Blakeboro' buildings
Tonge, Obadiah, Bradshawgate
Turner, James, Deansgate
Unsworth, Robert, Dawes' street
Vaughton, George, Hulme street
Vickers, Richard, Middle street
Vickers, John, Slater field
Vickers, Thos Ashburner street
Wadsworth, Thomas, Folds road
Wallwork, John, Nan lane
Walker, Cath. Market st., Farnh.
Walmsley, John, Ormrod street
Walmsley, Wm. Blackburn street
Walsh, James, York street
Warbury, George, Foundry street
Warburton Jacob, Harwood
Warburton Thomas, Kay st., L.B.
Warburton, Ellen, Brrdshawgate
Ward, John, Turton street
Warrington, Daniel, Churchgate
Webb, Martha, Ashburner street
Wilkins, Tim. King st., Farnwth.
Winters, Joseph, Little Lever
Whittaker, Wm. Bridgman street
Whitehead, Joseph, Folds road
Whiteside, M. 15 Howell croft
Whittle, James, Cannon street
Whittle, Christopher, Churchgate
Williams, Thomas, York street
Williams, Jane Weston street
Wilson, Mary, Deansgate
Windward, John, Sydney street
Winterbottom, J. Newport street
Wolfenden, Thomas, Brinks brow
Worsley, Wm. 37 Howell croft
Wright, Wm. Deansgate

Shuttle Makers.
Hargreaves, J. Commission street
Nicholson, James, 175 Kay street
Nicholson, Oliver, Blackburn st.
Rydings, Wm. Middle street

Sizers.
Rothwell, Wm. Hanover street
Sharples, Thomas, Bow street
Sharples, A. Independent street
Walmsley, Samuel, Spaw lane

Slate Merchants.
Gray, Amelia. Newport street and
Canal Wharf.—*See Advertisement*

Seddon, Henry & Eli, Bradshagt.
Walsh, James, Moor lane
Warr, Jonathan, & Son, Church
Wharf; *r* Back o'th bank; *r* Wharf

Slaters and Flaggers.
Brooks, Thomas, Mawdsley street
Gray, A. Newport street, & Wharf
Holland, Lewis, Bark street
Seddon, H. & E. Bridgman place
Walsh, James, Moor lane
Warr & Son, Church Wharf

Smallware Dealers
Ashall, William, Market street
Bradbury, Edward, Crown street
Goodfellow, S. New Market place
Hargreaves, Jno. White Lion brow
Jones, John, Deansgate
Salter, Sarah, Bradshawgate
Smith, J. (&Grocer) 9 Manor st.
Taylor, William, Deansgate
Taylor, Samuel, 4 Market street

Spindle Makers.
See also Roller Makers.
Albinson, John, Deansgate
Dobson & Metcalfe, Kay street
Hardman & Shepherd, Farnworth
Healey, John Grime st.; Office
Bark street; *r* Green hill
Knott, S. Taylor field ; *r* Green st.
Leyland, James, Crook street ; *r*
Commission street
Ryder, William, Bark street

Stationer—Wholesale.
Hughes, Robt. Exchange st. East
r Oxford street.—*See Advertisement.*

Stationer—Working.
Scholes, James, Shambles, *r* 21
Independent street

Stone Masons.
Crompton, J. 58 higher Bridge st.
Firth, James, Sharples
Gregson, Jonas, 184 Kay street
Hodkinson, Alexander, Kay street
Holland, Lewis, Bark street
Jackson, Robert, Mawdsley street
Seddon, H. & E. Bridgman place
Walsh, James, Moor lane

Stone Merchants.
Brocklebank, John, Canal Wharf
r Salford
Walsh, James, Moor lane

Straw Bonnet Makers.
Aspinall, M. A. Blackurn st. L.B.
Astley, Sarah, 80 Bark street
Baron, Jane, 102 Kay street
Chadwick, M. A. 64 Howell croft
Craigie, Mary, Bank street
Dixon, Jane, Foundry street
Graham, Mary Ann, 78 Kay street
Grundy, Anna, 85 Bridge street

Hancock, Rebecca, Folds road
Holt, Sarah, Mill street, L.B.
Howarth, Mary Ann, Moor lane
Johnson, H. Halliwell toll bar
Longworth, Mary, Bradshawgate
Metcalf, Frances, Market street
Naylor, Grace, Defence street
Ross, Robert, Bradshawgate
Rudd, Ellen, 3 Weston street
Shaw, Sarah, Back Oswald street
Thompson, Wm. New Mrkt.place

Stay Makers.
Atkinson, M. 10 Cheapside, and
  Deansgate, Manchester.—See Advertr.
Boyd, M. J. 96 Black horse street
Thompson, Wm. New Mrkt.place

Surgeons.
(See also Physicians.)
Anderton, G. L. Farnworth
Bancroft, Sifrid Nevil, Mawdsley st
Booth Thomas, Kearsley
Chadwick, S. T. Mancheter road
Denham, Joseph, Bridge street
Eames, T. B. Kearsley
Featherstonehaulgh, A. Barn st. L.B
Ferguson, Fergus, 19 Mawdsley st
Franklin, J. Belmont
Garstang, Thomas, Bark street
Haddock, Joseph W. (Surgeon-
  Apothecary) Cheapside
Hampson, Roger, Nelson square
Hatton, Henry, Bradshawgate
Lever, Joshua, Folds street
Mallett, George, 18 Mawdsley st.
Pendlebury, James, 30 Bridge st.
Rainforth, John, 108 Bark street
Robinson, John M. Bank house
Scowcroft, William, Churchgate
Seddon, John, Kearsley
Sharp, Henry, do.
Shaw, John, Edgeworth
Snape, Richd. Forth, Nelson sqr.
Watson, A. (& Apothecary) D'gate
Wolstenholme, Geor. St. Geo's. st

Tailors & Woollen Drapers.
(See also Tailors.)
Ackroyd, Samuel, 3 Deansgate
Ackroyd, Wm & Co. New Market
  Place, r Glocester Crescent London
Bridge, Wm. Derby street
Butler, Isaac, Acres' field
Fulton, Peter, Great Moor street
Greenhalgh, John, Farnworth
Greenlees, Samuel, Hotel street
Harkness and Charlton, Borough
  house, Market st.; r 79 Albert place;
  Derby street
Hesketh, William, Bradshawgate
Leyland, James, 4 Bridge street

Macoun, Henry, Hotel street
Marshall, John, Derby street
Payne, Wm. Deansgt. (See Advrt.)
Penney, William, Newport street
Quayle, Edward, Deansgate
Reddick, William, Knowsley street
Richardson, John, New Mrkt. plc.
Ridge, William, 156 Deansgate
Rothwell, Benjamin, Manor street
Saunders, William, Deansgate
Smith, William, Derby street
Smith and Brandwood, Derby st.
Sussum, G. 2 Bridge st; r Bath st.
Waring, John, Crown street
Watts, Alex. Deansgt. r Nelson sq
Wright, I. D'gate r Halliwell rd.

Tailors.
(See also Tailors and Woollen Draper)
Allen, William, King st. Farnwrth
Allison, Joseph, Kay street
Ashton, Wm. Blackburn street
Balshaw, James, Rothwell street
Barrow, John, Farnworth
Bennett, George, Chorley street
Booth, J. Newport street
Brenan, John, King st. Farnworth
Brooks, Fred. Union buildings
Brook, Thomas, Farnworth
Buckley, Thomas, Prestolee
Cartiner, George, Folds road
Clapham, James, Turton street
Coulston, Thos Blackhorse stree
Copley, Jeremiah, Velvet walks
Dodgin, John, 95, Turton street
Dingsdale, Christ, Old hall street
Fairclough, Richd. Mealhouse lane
Fletcher, James, Churchgate
Fletcher, John, Mill street
Fould, Robert, Derby street
Fulton, Peter, Gt. Moor street
Gibbin, P. back Shaw street
Greenhalgh, Joseph, Chapel st.
Greenhalgh, P. Bridgman place
Hughes, Jno. Bullock street
Hulton, Henry, Darcy Lever
Jackson, Richd. 28 Chancery lane
Karney, Patrick, Deansgate
Lawton, Rbt. Market st. Farnwth.
Layland, J. Bamber's crt. D'gate
Lever, James, Sydney street
Mc' Cabbe, James, Velvet walks
Mc' Donna, Maths. 123 Bridge st.
Marchbank, John, Middle street
Melville Geo. Commission street
Miller, John, 19 Bridge street
Moore, J. Ashburner, street
Myers, Wm. 51 Bow street

Nicholl, Robert, Turton street
Pearson, S. Nan lane, Farnworth
Penney, Thos Ainsworth
Plumbley, James, Halliwell
Proctor, John, All Saints street'
Raw, Wm. Nan lane, Farnworth
Richardson, J. Great Moor street
Ryland, John, Johnson street
Seddon, E. Cross Axe entry, D'gate
Sidlow, James, Kay street
Smith, J. Blackburn street, l.b.
Smith, David, Newport street
Storey, Joseph, Rothwell street
Thirlwind, John, Bank street
Thornley, James, Blkburn. st. l b.
Thwaites, Edwin, Bradshawgate
Travis, Daniel, Exchange street
Warbrick, R. Old Acres
Wilde, J. Folds road
Yates, Thos. Defence street

Tallow Chandlers
Hesketh, T. M. Bank street, and St. George's street
Smalley, Robert, Bradshawgate
Tickle, James, Bridge street

Tanners
Adamson, John, Chorley street, r Lodge Vale [r]Bury street
Briggs, Thomas, Church Wharf
Greenroyd, James, Bark bank l,b
Walker, W. & C. Stott billock

Taverns, Inns, &c.
See the Cover of the Almanack.

Tea and Coffee Dealers
Barlow, W. (&Tobacco) Oxford st.
Baron, T.   do   Bradshawgt.
Chorlton, John, Derby street
Dunderdale, Richd. 23 Deansgate
Haddock, Daniel, Oxford st.; r 18 St. George's terrace
Hamilton, J. Hotel st. r Rose hill
Healey, J. Deansgate, (opp. Black horse street)
Lord, Isaac, Independent street
Nicholson, John, & Co.(Liverpool Tea Company) Hotel street
Pendlebury, Samuel, 1 Market st: (Agent for Piqua Plant)
Steele, A. & N. 22 Deansgate
Stones, William, Deansgate
Rothwell, Jno. 17 Bridge street
Wright, Bro. & Co. (Wholesale) New Market place; r Mawdsley street

Temperance Hotels
Fishburn, Wm. Deansgate
Robinson, Wm. Howell croft
Seddon, Ann, Newport street
Stevenson, Matt. Folds road

TIMBER MERCHANTS & BUILDERS.
(See also Builders)
Almond & Norris, Bradshawgate
Barrow, Isaac, Deansgate
Bowen, and Brown, Blackurn st. r Moor lane
Blinkhorn Mary & Sons, Crown st
Cole, Thos. Newport street
Coope, Gideon, Farnworth
Crompton, Wm. Farnworth
Fowler, Luke, (& Saw Mills) 5 Knowsley street
Gawkroger, Geo. higher Bridge st.
Gent, Henry, Bradshawgate
Greenhalgh, Wm Johnson street
Haslam, Robert, Falcon street
Holt, John, Sharples
Hough, Richard, (Timber : & Saw Mills) Nelson square
Hurst, John, Moor lane
Lever, James, (Timber Merchant) Silverwell street; r Ringley
Marsden, James and Joseph, (Saw Mills) Deansgate and Bridge st; r 20 Chorley new road; r 15 St. Geor's. ter.
Shaw & Marsden, Taylor fold, r Brinks brow; r Shaw street
Tunstall, Jno. Little Hulton

Tobacco Manufacturers.
Baron, Thomas, jun. Barn street r 14 Green street
Johnson, John, Bradshawgate, r Victoria terrace
Johnson, Charles, Old hall street r Park hill
Tickle, James, Bridge street, r Tipping place

Tobacconists.
(See preceding List; also Tea dealers)
Baron, T. Bank street, r B'gate.
Fraser, John, Cheapside
Heyes, James, 43 Deansgate
Nuttall, E. and M. Churchgate

Tripe Dressers.
Haslam, R. and P. Deansgate
Haslam, Jon. Deansgate
Monks, John, Hulme street

Truss Maker.
Ainsworth, E. and Son, Barn str.

UMBRELLA MAKERS.
Harrison, Massah, Deansgate Folds road
Leach, Edward, Great moor street
Parr, J. Churchgate
Parkinson, W. D'gate & Folds road
Walsh, James, Kay street, l.b.

VETERINARY SURGEONS
Hampson, Roger, Nelson square
Knott, Daniel, Newport street
Lawson, A. Bradshawgate

WATCH AND CLOCK MAKERS.

Ashall, Wm. Market st. see Advt.
Ashall, Charles, Mealhouse lane
Aspinall, Wm. Great moor street
Berrington, John, Deansgate
English, D. Ashburner street
Herr, Joseph, Ashburner street
Isherwood, J. 42 Great moor street
Langley, Thos. Kay street, L.B.
Lee, Henry, Spring gardens
Lee, J. Kay street, L.B.
Manchester, Thos. Ridgway gates
Mancor, James, Bridge street
Monk, John, Deansgate
Tritchler, John, Bradshawgate
Tyson, Thomas, 8 Derby street
Wood, William, Old hall street
West, J. D'gate., corner of B'gate

WHEELWRIGHTS.
See also under title Blacksmiths
Baxter, John, Farnworth
Bentley, Thos. Harwood
Blackway, Wm. Blackburn st, L.B
  r Green street L B
Bridge, James, Tonge moor
Fletcher, L. Over Hulton
Hough, Richard, Nelson square
Morris, Wm. Blackburn street
Pollit, Thomas, Sydney street
Smith, G. Little Hulton
Swarsbrick, John, Hotel street

WINE, SPIRIT, & POR. MERCHANTS.

Bathe, Henry, Deansgate
Hall, Rowland, Nelson square
Loader, John, Bradshawgate
Paulton, Charles, 9 Folds street
Wallwork, Joseph, sen. Chapel st.
  r Chorley new road   [Chorley road
Wallwork, Rich. Bridge street ; r
Warburton, T. B'gate & Atherton,
  —See Advertisement   [Mawdsley st
Wingfield, T. Chancery lane , r

WIRE WORKER.
Cunliffe, Jno. Coope st. Newport st;
  r Folds road—See Advertisement

Wood Turners.
Draper, Thos. Salt pie factory, r
  20 Dawson lane
Hart, John, Cannon st. r Derby st
Rydings, Wm. Middle street
Singleton, Joseph, Blackburn str.

MISCELLANEOUS.
Allen, Jno. Carter, 21 Howell croft
Atherton, Jas. Skinner, Moor lane
Bate, James, Carter, Crook street
Bleakley, Wm. Billposter, York st
Chaplin, Jabez, Carpet warehouse,
  4 Deansgate
Cole, N. Berlin-wool deal. Newp. st
Craigie, C. Nurseryman, Chorley
Cross, R. Sexton, Shaw st. [road
Dorning, H. Clammerclough Pot-
  tery, Farnworth
Edwards, Edward, Coffee roaster
  and Chicory manufacturer, lower
  Nag's head yard.
Finnie, J. Cot.-sheet maker, Lever st
Foxon, C. Matron Lying-in Char.
Fraser, J. Commer. trav. Cheapsd.
Green, Hy. Carter, Chancery lane
Hall, J. Sexton, Bridge-st. chapel;
  r Ridgway gates
Haslam, P. Store kpr. mt. Pleasant
Hatton, T nail maker, Folds road
Holt, R. Malt grinder, Gleaves st
Horrocks, J. Sexton, Clarence st
Johnson, T. Toll kr Halliwell bar
Latham, W. Hackle mr. 172 Kay st
Longworth, J. Saw Mill, Taylor
  field, r Middle street   [Exchange st
Melling, T. Picture frame maker,
Pennington, H. Catl. dealer, B'gate
Philip, T. Last maker, Garside st.
Riley, John, Horse Shoer, Church-
  gate, r Naylor row
Rothwell, Ed. Store kpr. Derby st
Simpkin, J. Gun maker, chur. wrf.
Webster, J. Town missnry. Union st
Williams, J., road contractor
  Bridgman street
Wheatley, W. Druggist, &c, Kay st
Yates, R. Commer. trav. Bridge st

Reprinted in 1983 by
Neil Richardson, 375 Chorley Road, Swinton
ISBN 0 907511 17 1

£2.00